Book design for children's reading

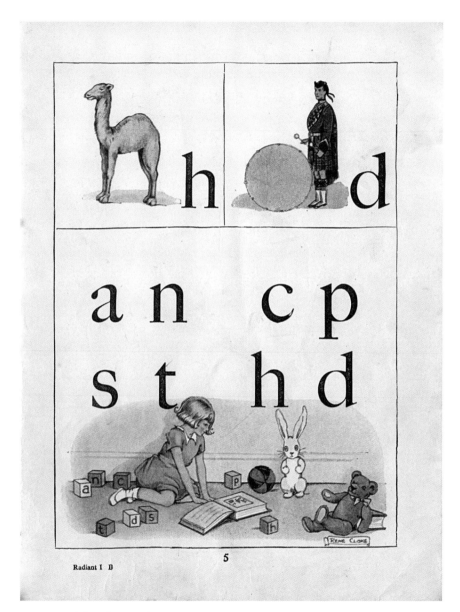

Jane Brown, 'The radiant way', *First step*,
Edinburgh and London: W. & R. Chambers,
1933, p. 5. Illustrated by Rene Cloke.

Sue Walker

Book design for children's reading

typography, pictures, print

St Bride Foundation, London

Published by the St Bride Foundation, London, 2013

This book was based on research undertaken
as part of the Typographic Design for Children
project at the Department of Typography & Graphic
Communication, University of Reading, funded by
the Arts and Humanities Research Council, UK.

The book was designed, typeset and made into
pages in Adobe InDesign by Sara Chapman,
Sandina Miller and Sue Walker. The text was set
in New Miller and Monotype Grotesque. The index
was made by Joan Dearnley, FSocInd.

Printed and bound in Oxford, UK
by Berforts Information Press.

ISBN 978-0-9504161-3-7

Contents

Foreword

The idea for this book arose during the 'Typographic design for children' project funded by the Arts and Humanities Research Council from 1999 to 2005. Several of the project outcomes – academic papers, publications for teachers and practitioners, a typeface, a research data base and a website – hinted at the potential for an illustrated historical account that raised the profile of a seemingly neglected area, the design of books for teaching young children to read. This account provides examples of books for teaching children to read in twentieth-century Britain and identifies factors that have influenced their visual appearance and the process of making them. Although a selective account, it aims to draw attention to the main organisational and stylistic changes of such books.

The illustrations in this book are from my collection, apart from those marked [DTC] or [BL] which are courtesy of the Department of Typography & Graphic Communication at the University of Reading or the British Library.

I would like to thank the following people for their advice and assistance in helping this book come to fruition: Polly Harte, Emma Minns, Alison Black, Paul Luna (especially for help in identifying typefaces), Rhona Stainthorp, Michael Twyman, Sandina Miller, Tess Millar, Martha Barratt, Amelia Barratt, Joan Dearnley, Viv Edwards, Sara Chapman, Emily Stannard, Glyn Farrow, Pankaj Vyas, the many people who have given me children's reading books, and the teachers and children that I have asked questions of over the years. I thank the authors, illustrators and publishers and others involved in the making of the books that I have discussed, and hope that I have acknowledged this work in full and in an appropriate way.

The book is being published by the St Bride Foundation in 500 copies; proceeds from the sale are going to support the work of the St Bride Library, in particular to help students access its outstanding typography and printing archives.

Sue Walker

3

Publisher's staff: *Cover* John Lewis and Peggy Beetles
Evans Bros.
Queensway Reading Books, Books 1–5, with *Words and Pictures*
by Mollie Brearley and Lois Nelson
Illustrator: Peggy Beetles
2s 3d to 3s 6d each
Letterpress
Balding & Mansell
John Dickinson & Co., Evensyde
Balding & Mansell, Durabak

4

Publisher's staff: *Cover* Sally Ford
Sir Isaac Pitman & Sons
ᚠe sæl awæ seerix
by Keith Gardner and Ulyth Roberts
Illustrator Sally Ford
Books 1 and 2, 4s; Book 3, 6s
Offset
Haycock Press
Book Papers, Keston Opaque Cartridge
Haycock Printers, Fabroleen

5

Publisher's staff. *Cover* A. R. Whitear and Patricia
Barton
Sir Isaac Pitman & Sons
ᚠe dounig reeders
by John Downing. *Illustrators* A. R. Whitear and
Patricia Barton
2s to 4s 6d each
Offset
Haycock Press
John Dickinson & Co., Regal and Evensyde
Cartridge
Haycock Press, Kinline and Coverdale

6

Publisher's staff. *Cover* Pamela Kington
Ginn & Co.
Fountain Picture Books, Books 1, 2, 3
by Jill Brandon and David Norris. *Illustrator*
Pamela Kington
3s 9d each
Offset
Curwen Press
John Dickinson & Co., Croxley White Offset
Curwen Press, Manilla

7

Publisher's staff. *Cover* Patricia McGrogan
E. J. Arnold
Penny at the seaside
by J. Havenhand. *Illustrator* Patricia McGrogan
3s
Offset
E. J. Arnold
Inveresk Paper Mill, Offset Cartridge
E. J. Arnold, Durabak

8

Publisher's staff *Cover* Peter Hardy
McDougall's Educational Co.
The eavesdroppers
by Tudur Watkins. *Illustrator* Paul Hogarth
5s
Offset
Banks & Co.
Inveresk Paper Mill, Printwell
Duncan & Son, Durabak

1 Spreads from *Textbook design exhibition 1966: catalogue of an exhibition of books published between May 1962 and May 1965*, London: National Book League, 1966, pp. [6–7] and [8–9]. Page 185 × 168 mm.

Winning examples of reading books selected by Ruari McLean, G. Fielden Hughes and Kenneth Pinnock.

Introduction

In 1966 an 'Exhibition of textbook design', organised by the London-based National Book League, displayed books chosen by G. Fielden Hughes, an education officer for Surrey County Council; Ruari McLean, a book designer; and Kenneth Pinnock, an educational publisher. They were asked to select the 'best designed' textbooks published between May 1962 and May 1965. Among these were some for teaching young children to read. The exhibition was accompanied by an illustrated catalogue, designed by McLean, showing covers and spreads of the chosen books and publishing and production details (1). The catalogue introduction included comments from each of the three selectors that highlight the particular relationship, in educational publishing, between pedagogy, design and publishing practice. Fielden-Hughes noted that the 'school book is the one agent of education which strikes the child in personal terms' and that 'no child can fail to be stimulated by books which have their own beauty and their own vivid appeal to the child's desire to learn'. The relevance of design was acknowledged by McLean: 'Textbooks need to be specially well-designed, for they must be approved twice: first by the school or educational authority that buys them; secondly by the student who has to read them'. But it was Pinnock who articulated the challenges:

> as an educational publisher ... I know how tempting it is to rely on precedent. With the established production formulae, one knows pretty much beforehand how estimates are going to turn out; the new paths always seem to lead to impossible published prices. Herein lies the great difference between educational and general publishing; all one's efforts and experiments are governed by what the schools will pay, all one's arts must be exercised within stringent limitations of price.[1]

He went on to say that educational publishers needed to be responsive to changes in education and in technology, noting that the pervasive use of offset lithography provided 'greater freedom in making layouts'; and that educational books were made up in publishing offices instead of being assembled by printers. He concluded that 'this new-found freedom ... has

1. *Textbook design exhibition 1966: catalogue of an exhibition of books published between May 1962 and May 1965*, London: National Book League, 1966, p. [3].

9

certainly led to some notable improvements in the art of presenting information clearly and attractively'.

Though children's books have been studied by scholars of literature, education, illustration, and history of the book, there is only occasional reference to books for teaching reading. Instead, in the words of Harvey Darton, they have concentrated on: 'printed works produced ostensibly to give children spontaneous pleasure, and not primarily to teach them'.[2] School-books, including those for teaching reading, are sometimes referred to in histories of publishing that highlight the importance of the education market in generating income;[3] or accounts that discuss authorship and content of texts used in teaching reading.[4] Histories written from an education perspective, such as Christopher Stray and Gillian Sutherland's recent account, and the earlier ones by Alec Ellis, mention books for teaching reading, usually in either the context of publishing or educational practice.[5] There has been some scholarly interest in books used for teaching reading in the United States, notably the work of Richard Venezky.[6] The journal of the Textbook Colloquium, *Paradigm*, contains a number of papers that look at reading primers used in different parts of the world, such as New Zealand and Australia.[7] Even when books for teaching reading are included, there has been little mention of their visual attributes, yet the accessibility and appropriateness of typography, illustration and materiality has to be a significant factor in determining whether or not a child is motivated to learn to read and helped in doing so.[8] Similarly these issues take a back seat in educational reports and books: comments tend to be slight, such as this rather sweeping, though not incorrect statement 'as long as the letters in early books are well-spaced and not too small, the typeface is not a serious matter.'[9]

2. F.J. Harvey Darton, *Children's books in England: five centuries of social life*, 3rd edn, revised by Brian Alderson, London and New Castle: British Library and Oak Knoll Press, 1999, p.1.

3. For example, Heather Holmes, and David Finkelstein (eds), *Thomas Nelson and Sons. Memories of an Edinburgh publishing house*, East Linton: Tuckwell Press, 2001, pp.xvii–xviii.

4. For example, Ian Michael, *The teaching of English from the sixteenth century to 1870*, Cambridge: Cambridge University Press, 1987.

5. Christopher Stray and Gillian Sutherland, 'Mass markets: education'. In *The Cambridge history of the book in Britain, vol. VI 1830–1914*, Cambridge: Cambridge University Press, 2009, pp.359–81; Alec Ellis, *A history of children's reading and literature*, Oxford: Pergamon Press, 1968; and Alec Ellis, *Books in Victorian elementary schools*, London: The Library Association, 1971.

6. Richard L. Venezky, 'A history of the American reading textbook', *Elementary School Journal*, vol. 87, no. 3, 1987, pp.246–64.

7. For example, Hugh Price, 'Lo, it is my ox!': reading books and reading in New Zealand Schools 1877–1900, *Paradigm*, no. 12, December 1993, pp.1–14 and P. W. Musgrave, 'Readers in Victoria, 1896–1968: the Victorian readers, *Paradigm*, no. 16, May 1995, pp.1–12.

8. This lack of attention is also evident in more general studies in book history so David McKitterick's chapter on 'Changes in the look of the book' in *The Cambridge history of the book in Britain*, 2009, pp.75–116 with sections on typesetting and type design, illustration, paper and book binding is a welcome addition and introduces these considerations of book design to a wider audience.

9. Margaret Meek, *Learning to read*, London: Bodley Head, 1982, p.46.

Books for teaching reading

This essay is about typography and the use of illustrations in reading books for young children. Teachers and educationists have played an important part in influencing the look and feel of these books. Their engagement, combined with craft tradition in the form of intervention by the compositor, printer or designer, and the economic and marketing concerns of the publisher, has resulted in the development of a clear typographic genre. In any period there is a 'typical look' for a school reading book created by its typefaces and their spacing, the relationship between text and illustrations, the format and the use of colour.

The books discussed here were produced from around 1890 to around 2000 by educational publishers for use in schools, primarily to teach reading to children aged between 4 and 7 in infant classes in primary schools in Britain and who can be described as 'beginner' or 'emerging' readers.[10] The term used to describe this stage of a child's education has varied over time. Today in England 'key stage 1' refers to primary school children between the ages of 5 and 7; in Scotland this stage is referred to as Primary 1, 2 and 3. Other terms used over the last hundred years were 'standard', 'grade' and 'level'. [11] Some reading book authors helpfully provided an indication of an age range for different levels of reading. Lucy Sidnell and Anne Gibbon, for example, in their series of 'fascinating readers for little ones' defined Grade 1 as 'suitable for advanced 5 year olds or early six year olds'.[12] A scheme of work for infant departments, approved by the Board of Education, reproduced in Gunn's *The infant school* (1906), related age to expected reading level within a series. According to John Gunn, a child aged 5 was expected to 'read with expression from Nelson's Royal King Infant Reader I'.[13] By the end of the nineteenth century books for teaching reading were usually produced in series where a book related to a stage or level in reading, and this continued through the twentieth century.

10. While this account is about books used in Britain for teaching reading, many British publishers produced books that were used overseas in India and Africa, for example. The reading book publishing industry in the USA had considerable influence on that in Britain, for example through the work of the publisher Ginn in the 1920s, and the introduction of the 'Janet and John' books in the 1940s.

11. See p.14 for a definition of 'standard' used at the end of the nineteenth century. Terminology for stages of a child's education varies from country to country.

12. Lucy Sidnell & Anne Gibbon, 'Wheaton's supplementary readers', *Stories of the seasons*, Exeter: A. Wheaton & Co, nd.

13. John Gunn, *The infant school: its principles and methods*, London: Thomas Nelson and Sons, 1906, p.399.

2 A spread from 'Cassell's modern school series', *Second infant reader*, London: Cassell & Company, 1886 showing examples of reading sheets. Page 170 × 114 mm.

This book comprises an 'introductory' section which includes reprints of the reading sheets that teachers would have used in the classroom, and 'reading lessons' formatted in two different ways.

The content of the books was usually narrative, often based around the lives of a particular group of characters, though non-fiction accounted for some strands within some reading series, such as 'object readers' at the end of the nineteenth century, and subject-specific books called history, geography or number readers. Many of the comprehensive reading schemes published in the 1980s and 1990s included non-fiction, and the book-banding approach taken in many contemporary schools includes non-fiction books at all reading levels.

In Britain there has never been a nationally-approved single method of teaching reading and there are no 'set books'. [14] It has been up to schools and teachers to choose which books to use in their classrooms (often within broad-based national guidelines, or from lists of recommended books for particular purposes and age groups). Particular reading book series or schemes would often be used in schools many years after their original publication date, which meant that some children learned to read from old-fashioned looking books, while others at a different school in the same town were learning with books recently published and acquired.

Reading books were often accompanied by various kinds of 'apparatus' to supplement the learning process. Reading charts, for example, were widely used in the nineteenth century, and sometimes reproduced in the book that accompanied them (**2**). Nellie Dale's approach to reading included the use of a tabulating frame, blackboards or slates and appropriate coloured chalks for the children to write with. [15] By the 1950s the 'reading scheme' was a popular notion in which a series of graded books was accompanied by reading cards, flash cards, supplementary

14. This is unlike many countries including the USA, Greece, Malaysia and China, where children use the same national, regional or state primer.
15. Nellie Dale, *On the teaching of English reading with a running commentary on the Walter Crane readers*, London: J.M. Dent & Co., 1898, pp.13–14.

Book design for children's reading

books, wall charts and pictures for copying and colouring in. However, criticisms of reading schemes in the Bullock Report, *Language for life* (1975)[16] encouraged schools to use books from more than one reading scheme and to make use of children's own writing as reading material. This view heralded the 'real books' approach to teaching reading where children chose what they wanted to read from books produced by both educational and trade publishers. By the end of the twentieth century children in many infant classrooms encountered a wide range of books, usually colour-coded according to reading level. In some schools where children spoke languages other than English, bilingual reading books became part of the mix, and growing awareness of different kinds of reading fuelled by National Curriculum guidance (1988) saw the introduction of 'big books' for group reading, and less of a separation between non-fiction and fiction books.

The analysis undertaken in this book surveys the visual attributes of over 1000 books used in Britain for the teaching of reading from the end of the nineteenth century to the beginning of the twenty-first.[17] Two factors influenced their inclusion: publication by a key educational publisher (such as Chambers, Blackie, Nelson, Collins, Ginn, Longman, Macmillan), or being listed in a publication that would have influenced the purchase of books for use in schools (such as the London County Council's *List of books, maps, music and diagrams approved for use in London schools maintained by the Council* which was published in numerous editions from the early 1900s until the 1950s). There has been little consistency in terminology for describing such books. In the nineteenth and early twentieth century, for example, the words 'primer' and 'reader' seem to have been used interchangeably: an 'infant reader' in one series might be at the same level of reading difficulty as a 'second primer' in another. 'Readers' or 'books' was used to describe a series of books: as 'Early steps readers' (1954) or 'The happy venture readers' (1945), as 'Books for me to read' (1964) or 'Playtime books' (1950). From the 1950s onwards nearly all books within series were given titles relevant to their content, rather than being designated *Book 1, Book 2* and so on.

I begin this account with a brief look at the situation at the end of the nineteenth century, in particular the consequences of the 1870 Education Act and the Revised Codes for publishers, that influenced publishing practice into the twentieth century. The second section has typography as its theme: typefaces and

16. The Bullock Report suggested that reading schemes should be developed without labels of 'look and say', 'phonic' etc. and should provide 'a sound basis for the development of all the reading skills in an integrated way'. Section 7.25 [accessed through D. Gillard, 'Education in England: a brief history', www.educationengland.org.uk/history]
17. The approach taken in this analysis is described in Sue Walker, 'Describing the design of children's books: an analytical approach', *Visible language*, vol. 46, no. 3, October 2012, pp. 182–201.

their spacing, and the influences on usage in books for teaching reading; and how typography has been used to differentiate component parts of text. Then the role of illustration and the relationship between text and pictures is discussed. Brief reference to cover design and variation across different editions precedes a short chronological overview of the main changes in visual organisation over this period. This is followed by an annotated visual 'timeline' that shows examples of reading books published in each decade from the 1890s until around the end of the twentieth century.

The situation at the end of the nineteenth century

The late nineteenth-century Revised Codes provide an example of the kind of impact that educational directives could have on the way books were used in the classroom, on their visual organisation, and on publishers' approaches to marketing. The Revised Code operated from 1862 until 1904, the result of recommendations made by the Newcastle Commission set up in 1858 to look into the provision of 'sound and cheap elementary education for all classes of people'. The most notable recommendation was that financial aid to schools should depend in part on attainment of pupils as measured by an inspector's examination in reading, writing and arithmetic: a system that became known as 'payment by results'.[18] Schools were subject to an annual inspection which looked at the levels of attainment in each of the prescribed Standards.[19] One consequence of the Revised Code was that teachers and children became dependent on the book used for teaching reading, and passages from it, even the whole book,

18. Schools were paid four shillings for every child in the school, plus two and eightpence per subject for every child who passed the annual examination in reading, writing and arithmetic. See Joachim M. Goldstrom, *Education: elementary education 1780–1900*, Newton Abbot: David & Charles, 1972, p. 126. Between 1862 and the end of the century there were numerous revisions and amendments, both to the Revised Code, and to instructions to Inspectors. Some of these, relevant to the use of books in schools, are summarised in Board of Education, *Books in public elementary schools*, 1928, pp. 8–13. (This was one of the five parts of the Hadow Report, published between 1923 and 1931. The 1928 review provided an historical perspective as well as a wide-ranging account of how books were used in schools.)

19. In 1862 these were set out as: Standard I, Narrative in monosyllables; Standard II, One of the narratives next in order after monosyllables in an elementary book used in the school; Standard III, A short paragraph from an elementary reading book used in the school; Standard IV, A short paragraph from a more advanced reading book used in the school; Standard V, A few lines of poetry from a reading book used in the first class of the school; Standard VI, A short ordinary paragraph in a newspaper or other modern narrative. Ellis, *Books in Victorian elementary schools*, 1971, pp. 41–2 lists the amendments to requirements in reading in 1871, 1873, 1875, 1879, 1880, 1882, and 1890.

Book design for children's reading

were learned by heart so that children did not fail in front of the Inspectors. As Richard Altick explained:

> And so bureaucracy, which then controlled the education of about two-thirds of all the children who were in school, prescribed the subjects each child was to take during a given year, the lesson books he was to study, and, most important of all, the nature of the examination to which he was to be subjected at the excruciating day of judgment, when every failure, per pupil, per subject, lost the school 2s.8d. from the next year's grant. The result was that a new premium was put on rote memory, for throughout the year every effort was bent toward grinding into the child the sentences or the facts that the inspector might demand of him. The best child (assuming he was not struck mute on examination day) was the one who had memorized the whole book).[20]

Many nineteenth-century reading books catered for more than one level of reading, with 'lessons' getting progressively more difficult (**3**). After 1862, and especially after 1870, rather than a single book divided into sections according to reading ability, the 'series' became a common mechanism for the publication of reading books. A series would contain volumes for infant primers, infant readers, and 'introductions to Standard I', and/or each of the Standards. The books were differentiated by content, and by appearance. Those in the infant classes and Standard I had larger type and more pictures than those in the higher Standards. In books for younger children (primers and Standards I and II) the Codes advised that:

> Two pages may be considered as the minimum for an effective reading lesson; and engravings, lists of words and names, and supplementary questions or exercises are not taken into account in computing the contents of the books, except to a small extent in the First Standard.[21]

As a result, primers began to be broken down into two- or three-page sections that typically contained a list of new words, a picture, a series of numbered paragraphs followed by a word exercise and some letters or words for writing practice as shown in Figure **4**.

The Revised Codes as well as the 1870 Education Act had considerable impact on the publishing industry, as noted by Alistair McCleery in his introduction to the Thomas Nelson and Sons company history:

20. Richard D. Altick, *The English common reader*, Chicago: University of Chicago Press, 1957, p. 157.

21. *Books in public elementary schools*, 1928, p. 11. This is cited from Circular No. 228 published by the Education Department in 1883, and repeated as a paragraph in *Revised instructions to H. M. Inspectors* in 1890.

3 Spreads from 'Blackie's comprehensive school series', *Primer. Part 1*, London: Blackie & Son, 1879, pp. 4–5, 10–11, 28–9. Page 164 × 112 mm.

The lessons in this primer increase in difficulty throughout the book, beginning with alphabets and common combinations of letters, progressing to short sentences using 2- and 3-letter words, to longer sentences introducing 4- and 5-letter words. As the text becomes more difficult, the type is reduced in size and the amount of text on a page increases.

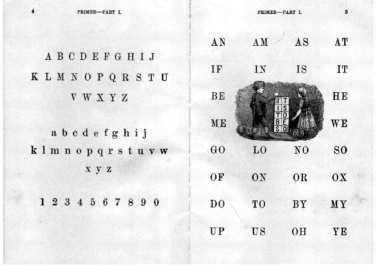

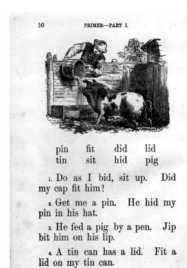

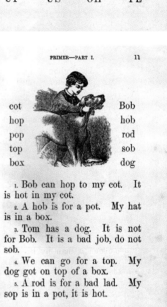

4 Spread from the 'Royal school series', *The Queen infant reader*, London and Edinburgh: T. Nelson & Sons, 1880s, pp. 10–11. Page 162 × 106 mm.

An example of a typical Revised Code reader: the main text broken down into numbered paragraphs, a title in capital letters, a list of new words, a word or spelling exercise and a handwriting specimen. The book was made up of short sections containing these elements, often presented as double-page spreads.

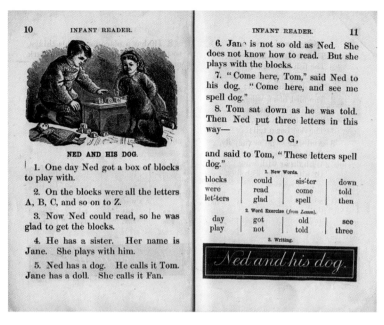

The various Education Acts after 1870 stimulated a tremendous demand for learning materials and Nelsons responded with the 'Royal Readers' series which sold in vast quantities throughout the British Empire. The Royal Readers were followed by the 'Royal School' series which eventually included some seventy titles. A watching brief was kept conscientiously on the market: the company corresponded with educationalists; it maintained contacts with school boards, at home and abroad, seeking always to answer particular needs; and the products of rivals such as Blackie and Arnold were monitored. Between 1878 and 1881 educational titles represented 25 per cent of the total output of Nelsons but yielded 88 per cent of the company's total profit.[22]

Collins's catalogues also showed an increase in school-book titles from 571 in 1865 to 920 in 1875, and Alec Ellis noted that they had to install new printing presses in order to cope with demand.[23] The phrase 'specially adapted to the Revised Code' began to appear in the titles of reading books, and publishers competed to produce material in accordance with government legislation. To sell their books, especially as educational texts were a lucrative revenue stream, publishers had to think of ways to draw attention to their version of the prescribed elements. They distinguished their books visually, some through typography, others through illustration (**5**), and made much of this in supporting publicity. Publishers' advertisements were rich in

22. Holmes and Finkelstein, *Thomas Nelson and Sons. Memories of an Edinburgh publishing house*, 2001, pp. xvii–xviii.

23. Ellis, *A history of children's reading and literature*, 1968, p. 91.

Educational publishers at the end of the nineteenth century competed to make their books visually distinctive. 'Macmillan's new literary readers' used an attractive and consistent style of illustration. 'Longmans' new readers' used somewhat eccentric typography to promote a 'look and say' approach to the teaching of reading.

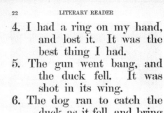

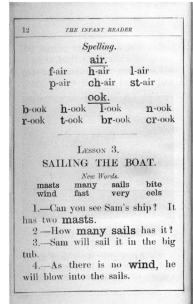

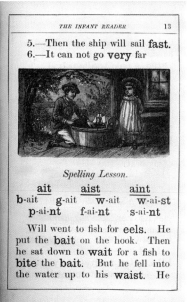

comments about visual appearance: illustrations, binding, paper quality, page size and typeface, and reflected fierce competition. Publishers advertised in magazines and journals, such as a prospectus for 'Murby's consecutive narrative reading books' (1870s) which explained that:

> No pains or expense have been spared in the preparation of the series; which, in the several points of illustration, typography, paper, and binding, will be found of the very best description. This has somewhat enhanced the price, but it will be found to compare favourably with that of other houses for work of the same excellent character.

6 Detail from a 'Prospectus' that appeared as a '*Good Words* advertising sheet', 1 January 1870. Page 245 × 167 mm.

This shows the typography used in each of the books in the series 'Murby's consecutive narrative reading books'.

SPECIMENS OF THE TYPOGRAPHY.

[FIRST READER—PART I.]

A PIG IN A BAG.

bad   pet   pig   got

A pig ran by us. A man had put him in a bag, and he got out.

Was it bad to try to get out? Get out of a bag if you can, so say I. Who may say No to a pig? It is of no use

[FIRST READER—PART II.]

Chap. VIII.—Claws.

[Spell :—*Sharp, tight, hurt, bleed, cross, nurse, smack, catch, mouse, spring*.]

"Take care, Hu, dear, or puss will hurt you with her sharp claws. She does not like to be held so tight."

"I want to pat her, I do not wish to hurt her. Why should she hurt me?" said Hu to his mam-ma.

"There, now; puss has made your hand bleed. Go, you cross

[SECOND READER.]

CHAP. XVII.

Liz Brown.

[Spell :—*al'-ways, knit, i'-dle, be-cause', ti'-dy, mo'-ther, teach'-er, school*.]

LITTLE Liz Brown, of the mill, was one of the best girls at school. She did not miss a day if she could help it, once in the whole year; and her tasks

[THIRD AND FOURTH READERS.]

CHAPTER XXXVIII.

THE FORGE.

[Spell :—*ear'-li er, pro-posed', re-sem'-blance, trou'-ble-some, cru'-ci-ble, cer'-tain-ly, dur'-a-ble, dif'-fer-ence, ar'-sen-al, ed-u-ca'-tion, man'-a-ger*.]

HU'S father came home earlier than usual, to see Aunt Mea and her boys; and finding them a little saddened by the morning's affair, proposed to take them a walk into the woods before tea.

[FIFTH AND SIXTH READERS.]

CHAPTER LVII.

THE RIDE TO THE FAIR.

Mag-ni'-fi-cent, splendid ; *im-pos'-si-ble*, not to be done ; *An-da-lu'-si-ans*, coming from Andalusia in Spain ; *des-pic'-a-ble*, worthy of contempt.

COWARDICE is a selfish and despicable sentiment, but timidity is not inconsistent with the highest acts of heroism and self-

Figure **6** shows examples of the typography from each volume in the series, illustrating a reduction in the type size through the various reading levels.

By the last decades of the nineteenth century, then, educational publishers had responded to growing demand for reading books that conformed to educational policy directives. They had begun to exploit two important 'tools of their trade': the craft tradition of the compositor, and new developments in printing, particularly the use of colour to differentiate their books from their competitors. There was some evidence of responsiveness to teacher suggestions regarding visual attributes that would help young children learn to read. Throughout the twentieth century pedagogy became increasingly influential in determining the visual organisation of reading books as did greater collaboration between teachers, publishers and printers. This is seen in two main areas: typefaces and their spacing, and the way that text and pictures were used to inform and motivate young readers.

7 Spread from 'Little tales for Jack and Jill', *A. 16 The willow rod*, London: Collins Cleartype Press, [1920s], pp. [2–3]. Page 192 × 144 mm.

Large type with tight line spacing and justified setting results in a page with variable word spacing that interrupts the horizontal flow of the type.

go at once and get a rod to beat you."

Off she went to the willow tree.

"Do you want a rod?" said the willow tree.

"Yes," said Nell, "I want a rod to beat Ned, who ate up all my berries."

"You cannot have me," said the rod, "till you get an axe to cut me."

Nell came to the axe.

"Do you want an axe?" said the axe.

"Yes," said Nell, "I want an axe, an axe to cut the rod, the rod to beat Ned, who ate up all my berries."

"You cannot have me," said the axe, "till you get a stone to put an edge on me."

8 Spread from 'Gibson's simplified print writing primer', *Stage 3*, Glasgow: Robert Gibson & Sons, 1920s, pp. 18–19. Page 190 × 136 mm.

Although this primer is set in sanserif type, the visual organisation is reminiscent of books published at the end of the nineteenth century: justified setting to the full page width, numbered paragraphs, word lists, running headlines and decorative use of colons and rules which results in a cluttered page.

18   The lost six-pence.

6. "Gee up, hors-es!" and Tom crack-ed his whip to make them go fast-er.

7. But a pur-se is not like a whip; it can o-pen.

8. Just then, the spring lost its catch, and the six-pen-ce shot o-ver the top of the bridge in-to the riv-er.

9. Alas! it was quite lost.

10. Moth-er was sad to think her lad was so care-less.

11. Tom made up his mind to do bet-ter next time.

12. Sin-ce then, he has lost no more six-pen-ces.

The blind girl.   19

Vowel long before **nd, ld,** and **gh** silent.

Drill.

find	old	high	light
blind	bold	sigh	sight
wild	sold	might	tight
child	told	night	fright

Practice.

Ma-ry	school	smile-d
there	step-ped	less-ons
where	for-ward	gen-tle-man

: Story 6. :: The blind girl. :

Look and say—**eyes.**

1. Is it not sad to be blind!

2. This lit-tle girl can-not see the sun-light or the sky.

3. But still she is bright and cheery. Her name is Ma-ry. Has she not a nice face?

9 Spread from 'The new beacon readers', *Introductory book*, London: Ginn & Company, 1922, pp. 28–9. Page 183 × 132 mm.

The books published by Ginn, influenced by practice in the USA, anticipate the typical visual characteristics of many twentieth-century reading books: ranged-left setting with generous space between words and lines, ample page margins, and illustrations relevant to the text positioned below them.

28

Rover likes to play ball.

Do you like to play ball?

I have a ball.

It is a pretty ball.

Have you a ball?

Do you like to play with it?

Yes, I like to play with my ball.

29

See the little kitty.

It is John's little kitty.

John likes his little kitty.

His kitty likes Ruth, too.

Ruth is John's sister.

Have you a sister?

Yes, I have a little baby sister.

Do you like your little sister?

Yes, I do like my baby sister.

Typography for children's reading

Books for beginner readers involve the design of relatively short pieces of continuous text, and sometimes the differentiation of other elements that relate to it, such as lists of new words and spelling exercises. In most cases the typography is plain and straightforward though there are examples of relatively complicated-looking pages, particularly in books published in the first half of the twentieth century. One reason for this was that the type was often large relative to the page size, set with tight line spacing. The practice of justifying lines of type so that the right–hand edge was straight resulted in extremely variable word spacing, especially so because words were rarely hyphenated at the ends of lines. The word spacing was frequently wider than the line spacing which, as seen in Figure **7**, interrupted the horizontal flow of the lines of type. The treatment of elements such as lists of new words, word-drills and instructions to teachers sometimes added to the visual confusion as in the primer published by Robert Gibson shown in Figure **8**. The use of the double-page spread as a 'container' for text and pictures relating to a reading lesson, or a page or spread as a semantic unit in which text and illustrations were in close alignment, became increasingly typical from the 1920s onwards as in the picture/text configuration shown in 'The new beacon readers' in Figure **9**.

Decisions about typography were taken by publishers and printers drawing on precedent, educational directives, teachers' opinions and interpretations of legibility research relevant to children's reading. Each of these factors influenced the visual organisation of reading books leading to considerable variation in typography and layout, both synchronously and over time. A particular printer's stock of typefaces and a publisher's desire to follow precedent may have accounted for the continued use of modern-face type well into the twentieth century, for example. Some publishers and printers may have been influenced by type manufacturers' publicity and purchased one of the new Monotype typefaces marketed for school-book use in the late 1920s, or other typefaces that they thought would encourage schools to use their books. From time to time typefaces have been designed specially for children, such as Augmented Roman in the 1960s, the Sassoon family of typefaces and publisher-commissioned fonts such as those used by Oxford University Press and Heinemann from the 1980s onwards. Some typographic decisions were influenced by teaching practice, such as the linking of sanserif typefaces with handwriting teaching in the 1920s and 1930s.[24] Books for teaching reading have also been the subject of legibility and linguistic research and this, to a greater or lesser extent, has had an impact on their visual organisation.

School hygiene and legibility research

At the end of the nineteenth century psychologists and medical practitioners began to be interested in issues of 'school hygiene', in particular the effect of reading and writing upon eyesight.[25] This led to recommendations for the use of particular kinds of typeface, type size and spacing in books for beginner readers, such as those from James Kerr who wrote:

> With English type the only troubles likely to arise are from fine type, from the lines being too long, and insufficiently leaded, and from the paper being finished with a glossy surface. The *type* should be clear and large, and the construction of such letters as *h* and *b*, *v* and *n* should be especially precise.[26]

Similar ideas were presented in books written for teachers, such as John Gunn's *The infant school* (1906), where the author argued that suitable typefaces should 'have good proportions, with not too much difference between the thickness of its different parts, and plenty of "daylight" in its openings and curves'. [27] Gunn translated this generality into a specimen of type entitled 'Early reading lessons', showing an old-style typeface taken from the 'King infant' series, published by Nelson (who also published Gunn's book) (**10**). This suggests there may have been dialogue between author and publisher, or that Gunn took advice from

24. See Sue Walker, 'Letterforms for handwriting and reading: print script and sanserifs in early twentieth-century England', *Typography Papers 7*, London: Hyphen Press, 2007, pp. 81–114.

25. Summaries of eye-movement and other psychological reading research are given in Richard L. Venezky, 'The history of reading research.'

In: D. P. Pearson, R. Barr, M. L. Kamil and P. Mosenthal, *Handbook of reading research*, 1, London: Longman, 1984, pp. 3–38. See also Lynne Watts and John Nisbet, *Legibility in children's books: a review of research*, Slough: NFER Publishing Company, 1974, and summaries in Cyril Burt 'The typography of children's books: a record

of research in the UK.' *Yearbook of Education*, 1960, pp. 242–56.

26. James Kerr, 'Eyesight in school life'. In Arthur Newsholme & Walter C. Pakes, *School hygiene: the laws of health in relation to school life*, London: Swan Sonnenschein & Co, 1904, p. 94.

27. Gunn, *The infant school*, 1906, p. 162.

Book design for children's reading

10 Type specimen shown in John Gunn, *The infant school*, London: Thomas Nelson & Sons, 1906, p. 255 (top) and spread from 'The royal king infant reader', *No. 2*, London: Thomas Nelson & Sons, 1903, pp. 14–15. Page 172 × 129 mm.

The specimen shows the type recommended for early reading books. Gunn wrote: 'The size is sufficient, and the form is open and well-proportioned, without excessive contrast between the thick and the thin parts, and without the heaviness of some types which are used for the sake of clearness. The large specimen represents the same type enlarged five times, for use in reading sheets. The specimens are selected from the "King" Infant Series of the publishers of this book.'

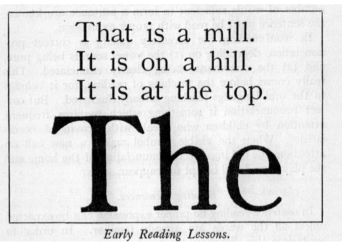

Early Reading Lessons.

28. Typography in school books had been a topic of interest at BAAS meetings since 1903 (see Walker, 'Letterforms for handwriting and reading', 2007). The content of the 1913 report was heavily influenced, even down to similarity of phrasing, by Edmund Huey, *The psychology and pedagogy of reading with a review of the history of reading and writing and of methods, texts and hygiene in reading*, New York: Macmillan, 1908, [2nd edn 1968 MIT Press]). Huey summarised findings of psychologists and vision scientists and related this to educational practice.

29. British Association for the Advancement of Science, *Report on the influence of schoolbooks upon eyesight*, London: John Murray, 1913, pp. 13–14. A summary of the other recommendations is given in the Appendix on p. 196.

the printers of the Nelson series about which typefaces to use. At this time, old-style typefaces were beginning to replace the modern-face types common in late nineteenth-century readers, so Gunn's inclusion was up to date.

The recommendations that had the most impact on typography in books for teaching reading in the first half of the twentieth century were those published in 1913 by the British Association for the Advancement of Science (BAAS) in their *Report on the influence of schoolbooks upon eyesight*.[28] Prescriptions for type size, line spacing and length of line in relation to age were given in a 'Standard typographic table' and illustrated in a series of 'Specimens of type', two of which are shown in Figure **11**. The strongest recommendation was that 'the size of the type-face is the most important factor in the influence of books upon vision'.[29] The table, however, also provided

11 Two of the type specimens from the Supplement to the British Association for the Advancement of Science *Report on the influence of school-books upon eyesight,* London: John Murray, 1913, pp. 24–31. Reproduced actual size.

No. 2.

UNDER SEVEN.

This type may be used for books to be read by children under seven. The letters are larger than the minimum given in the typographical table. Printed from 24 Point Old Style.

No. 4. AGE SEVEN TO EIGHT

This type may be used for books to be read by children from seven to eight years old. The letters are larger than the minimum given in the typographical table. Printed from Eighteen Point Old Style Antique.

suggestions for 'minimum interlinear space', and while acknowledging that too little space between the lines was a 'source of fatigue' in reading, the authors of the report thought that very wide spacing had no advantage and led to waste of paper and an increase in the number of pages. The 1913 *Report* had considerable influence; it was publicised widely in educational and printing journals, and the inclusion of 'printing experts' on the committee that compiled it is likely to have added to its credibility amongst printers and publishers. Compositors and printers may have seen reference to it in Legros & Grant's *Typographical printing surfaces* (1916).[30] John H. Mason summarised it in 'The printing of children's books' in *The Imprint* in 1913. Teachers may have read about it in educational journals, such as *School World* or *The Practical Teacher* and in publishers' publicity material.[31] Just as their nineteenth-century counterparts had drawn attention to their adherence to the Revised Code, several publishers acknowledged the 1913 *Report* in their publicity and notes to teachers. Blackie was one publisher that included such a comment on the inside back cover of 'Blackie's new systematic English readers', *First infant reader, c.*1913:

> An entirely new departure has been made in *format*, a large page with large type well spaced having been adopted in full conformity with the recommendations of the British Association Committee specially appointed to enquire into the print of schoolbooks in relation to eyesight.

The Scottish publisher, Robert Gibson, in relation to their 'Simplified print writing primers' also referred to conformity to the *Report*'s recommendations on the arrangement and size of type even though it was set in a sanserif typeface.

From the 1910s until the 1930s the influence of the work of the BAAS and legibility researchers was shown through a growing use of old-style, or old-style bold typefaces, and in the use of large type sizes with very tight line spacing (**12**). The BAAS *Report* had considerable reach in other ways: it influenced the development of Century Schoolbook, a typeface first issued and used by the publisher Ginn for the 'Beacon' reading scheme in the USA. Paul Shaw in his account of the design of the typeface noted that the designer, Morris Fuller Benton:

> consulted the 'Report on the Influence of School Books upon Eyesight' written for the British Association for the Advancement of Science, and other academic studies on the subject. All of these tests and experiments indicated

30. Lucien A. Legros and John C. Grant, *Typographical printing surfaces*, London: Longmans, Green & Co, 1916, pp. 157–60.

31. See, for example, 'Eyesight and typography', *The School World*, October 1912, pp. 382–7.

12 Examples of spreads from books produced in line with recommendations in the BAAS *Report on the influence of schoolbooks upon eyesight* (1913).

The top two examples show the common practice of increasing type size without a corresponding increase in line spacing. Combined with justified setting without word breaks which resulted in variable word spaces, it meant that in many cases the horizontal flow of type was disrupted.

Eleanor Chambers, 'Blackie's new systematic English readers', *First infant reader*, London and Glasgow: Blackie, 1906, pp. 44–5; one of a series published between 1913 and 1924. Page 205 × 135 mm.

E. A. Gregory 'New steps for tiny folk', *Two little runaways*, London: Oxford University Press, *c.*1926. Page 185 × 145 mm.

'Chambers's phonic and effective series', *Chambers's first primer*, London and Edinburgh: W. & R. Chambers, 1920, pp. 4–5. Page 198 × 140 mm.

This example follows the recommend-ation of large type and 'well-spaced' type which 'necessitated the use of a comparatively large size of page, but one not, it is hoped, beyond the capacity of little hands to hold.'

5. Now, he could sell the shoes, and get more skin. And he did so. Then he cut out fresh shoes from the skin, and left them in the middle of the bench.

6. In the morning they were done as before; so he sat up, to watch who made them.

7. He saw a little elf, only ten inches tall, tapping at the shoes, but he had no jacket on.

8. Then the cobbler cut out a jacket; stitched it up; put gilt buttons on it; and left it on the bench for the elf.

9. The little man was so glad. He put the jacket on; and then he danced all over the bench, singing,
"Now I have a red wool jacket,
I must not work, lest I should black it."

10. So the elf made no more shoes; but, still, the cobbler got on well after that.

—Old Scotch Story.

Ducky Lucky," they said. "Will you bring a pail and come to play and dig on the sands with us?"

"No," said Ducky Lucky. "I cannot come to play and dig on the sands with you to-day. I cannot run as fast as you can. I shall stay and swim in this pond with my little ducklings."

So off ran Sam and Pip to play and dig on the sands.

III
On the way they met a robin.

"Hullo, little robin," said Sam and Pip. "We are running away to play with this pail and dig on the sands to-day. Will you come with us, little robin?"

"No," said Baby Robin. "I must stay in the nest and wait till my mother comes

4

an   man   tan   Dan   to
can   pan   van   Fan   the
fan   ran   and   Nan

1. The man in a van is Dan.
2. Nan ran up to the van.
3. Nan can fan Dan.
4. The fan is on the can.
5. The can is in the pan.
6. Fan ran to Dan and Nan.
7. Fan is at the van; Nan is in the van.

5

at   cat   hat   pat   sat
bat   fat   mat   rat   Pat

1. A fat cat sat in a van.
2. The fat cat sat on a mat.
3. A rat ran in-to the van.
4. The fat cat ran at the rat.
5. The rat ran in-to a can.
6. The cat is at the can.
7. Nan can pat the fat cat.
8. Pat sat on a bat in the van. Fan sat on a mat.

13 Detail showing Century Schoolbook used in 'The new beacon readers', *Book one*, London: Ginn and Company, 1922, pp. 2–3. Reproduced actual size.

Kitty is in my lap.
See baby pat the kitty.
Baby says, "Kitty, little kitty."
It is a fat little kitty.
Baby likes to pat the kitty.
Mother, do see baby and kitty.

that children required larger and more distinct typefaces than did adults. Consequently, Benson increased the space between the letters, the x-height of each letter, and the weight of each stroke, and balanced the colour of the type by opening up the counters. The result was Century Schoolbook, completed in 1919, a face that is sturdier and more open than Century.[32]

Century Schoolbook first appeared in the UK in the 'New beacon readers', published by Ginn in 1922 (**13**).[33] It was subsequently used by several leading educational publishers including Nelson for 'The McKee readers' (*c.*1955); Harrap for the 'Peter and Mary' series (1940), Nisbet for the 'Janet and John' books (1949) and Oliver & Boyd for 'The happy venture readers' in the mid-1940s.

Printing industry interest and influence

There was some interest in what typefaces should be used for schoolbooks (including reading books) in printing journals in the 1930s. David Thomas in *Printing Review* questioned why educational publishers paid so little attention to typography.[34] He presented his perception of the publisher as: 'I dare not alter the style of a selling line that keeps me in business, as well as my father, and his father before him'; and of the experimental psychologist 'who has researched so much and discovered so little'. Thomas went on to recommend Garamond and Plantin set in 14-point or above for children under eight; and Caslon, Old Style, Old Face, Imprint and Baskerville as typefaces '*par excellence*' for children between eight and fourteen years old. Robert D. Morss, Managing Director of Ginn, also approved of these typefaces and wrote in 1935 in the *Monotype Recorder* to promote

32. Paul Shaw, 'The Century family', in Charles Bigelow, Paul Hayden Duensing and Linnea Gentry (eds), *Fine print on type*, San Francisco: Bedford Arts, 1989, p. 49.

33. The scheme was introduced in England by Robert D. Morss who was appointed in 1919 to rejuvenate the company (see Thomas Lawler, *Seventy years of textbook publishing: a history of Ginn and Company*, Boston: Ginn and Company, 1938, p. 114 and, for a summary of Ginn's reading program in the USA, pp. 187–90). Morss went on to work closely with Beatrice Warde on publicising Monotype typefaces suitable for children's reading (Walker, *Letterforms for handwriting and reading*, pp. 100–101).

34. David Thomas, 'School books and their typography', *Printing Review*, vol. 13, 1934, pp. 5–8.

14 From R. D. Morss, 'The neglected schoolbook', *Monotype Recorder*, 1935, vol. 34, p. [7]. Reproduced actual size.

Specimen showing 'adequately leaded and spaced' type for particular age groups; set in Monotype Baskerville. Along with Baskerville, the other Monotype faces shown in Morss's illustrations are Century Schoolbook, Plantin 110 and Imprint 101.

Adequately leaded and spaced, these

GRADATIONS

OF TYPE SIZE ARE APPROPRIATE

for the reading matter of children aged

from 6 to 7 years

a clean clear open appearing type is both an invitation and an en-

from 7 to 8 years

a clean clear open appearing type is both an invitation and an en-

from 8 to 9 years

a clean clear open appearing type is both an invitation and an encourage-

from 10 to 12 years

a clean clear open appearing type is both an invitation and an encouragement to the young reader

from 12 to 15 years

a clean clear open appearing type is both an invitation and an encouragement to the young

Fig. 5

newly-cut Monotype faces. He provided a type specimen showing typefaces 'adequately leaded and spaced' (**14**). Morss also made a plea that greater resource for schoolbooks be made available in response to a comment in the 1928 Hadow Report that it was 'seriously insufficient'. He went on to refer to the influence of the 1931 Hadow Report that advocated the notion of education as an active process and argued that this was leading to a demand for:

> a new type of school book, a book that will be so interesting and attractive that the pupil, no matter how limited or unfortunate his home surroundings, will regard it with delight. These new school books, if they are to become an

effective instrument of social service, will be written and produced for the child, rather than to meet a formal examination requirement.[35]

Morss, then, was one of a growing contingent who thought it important to prioritise the reading needs of children. His article, profusely illustrated with pages of books set in Monotype fonts, stressed the importance of the role of the publisher in achieving high quality levels, and in bringing together all the specialisms involved in the production of a book: author, typographer, printer, binder, paper-maker and illustrator. His article was well received and according to Beatrice Warde, publicity manager at Monotype, aroused considerable interest. Morss also referred to the impact of the Monotype Large Size composition equipment that ensured 'clean clear types' for children's books, a point also made by Beatrice Warde in the same issue:

> The Large Size Composition equipment on 'Monotype' machines makes it unnecessary to resort to the use of worn type and hand-setting for a child's book in sizes large enough for unaccustomed eyes. The growth of publicity material has greatly increased the amount of large size composition done, and at the request of printers here and abroad a large majority of the classic 'Monotype' faces now possess 16 or 18 or 24-point composition matrices.[36]

The availability of typefaces in large sizes increased the range used in children's books and from the 1930s Imprint, Baskerville, Plantin, Century Schoolbook and Gill Sans were often selected for use in reading books.

Influence of the teaching of handwriting

Some teachers thought that handwritten letterforms, rather than typefaces, were more appropriate for children leaning to read. In the 1920s the keen interest of many teachers in the print script approach to teaching handwriting encouraged some to produce their own reading books using such letterforms.[37] These letters were often ill-formed and quirky such as those in the 'Seandar' series' (*c*.1929) where the ascenders and descenders were extremely long (**15**). 'Blackie's coloured manuscript readers', published in the 1920s, used the letterforms devised by the teacher, S. A. Golds, and presented in her book *A guide to the teaching of handwriting* (1919). These had a soft, informal feel (**16**). Though many of the books with handwritten letterforms were originally

35. Robert D. Morss, 'The neglected schoolbook', *Monotype Recorder*, vol. 34, no. 2, 1935, pp. 7–9.

36. Beatrice Warde, 'Annual or perennial? The problem of producing books for young readers', *Monotype Recorder*, vol. 34, no. 2, 1935, p. 16. Warde lists the 'large size' Monotype faces available: Baskerville 169, Bodoni, Caslon, Fournier, Garamond 156, Imprint 101, Centaur, Lutetia, Poliphilus and Blado, Verona, Horley Old Style, Gill Sans 262, Bembo, and Plantin 110. She does not include Century Schoolbook, but this is shown in 18-point in Morss's paper in the same issue of the *Monotype recorder*.

37. See Walker, 'Letterforms for handwriting and reading', 2007.

15 Spread from 'The "Seandar" individual reading books', *My first reading book*, Leeds: E. J. Arnold, *c*.1929/30, pp. 8–9. Page 183×139 mm.

An example of 'print script' letterforms used in a reading book, a practice favoured by some teachers.

16 Spread from Lucy Maria Sidnell & Anna Maria Gibbons, 'Blackie's coloured manuscript-writing infant readers', *Little ones' own picture reader*, London and Glasgow: Blackie & Son, 1924, pp. 26–7. Page 187×140 mm. [BL]

This series used the letterforms shown in S. A. Golds, *A guide to the teaching of manuscript writing*, London: Blackie & Son, 1919 and *Blackie's manuscript writing copy-books, nos 1–6*, London: Blackie & Son, *c*.1920s.

published by small local publishers, some found their way on to mainstream publishers' lists. E. J. Arnold, for example, took over the publication of the Seandar series from Cartwright and Rattray, a small publisher based in Hyde, and the series continued to be produced until at least the end of the 1930s.

Since the 1920s and 1930s, the use of handwriting in reading books has been infrequent, with two notable exceptions. The first books for beginners in 'The Ladybird key words reading scheme', published from 1964, used a handwritten letterform with long ascenders and descenders (**17**). It is likely that some form of stencil was used in the production process because there is very little difference between the individual letterforms, but variation in horizontal space. In the 1980s, the 'Oxford reading tree', used handwriting which was also very well received by children and teachers (**18**). Both the Ladybird and Oxford

17 Spread from William Murray, 'The Ladybird key words reading scheme', *2b Have a go*, Loughborough: Ladybird Books, 1964, pp. 28–9. Page 171 × 112 mm.

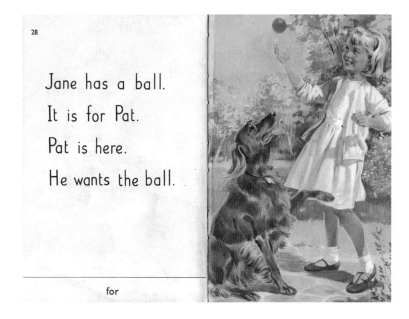

18 Spread from Roderick Hunt, 'Oxford reading tree', *What a bad dog!*, London: Oxford University Press, 1986, pp. 12–13. Page 192 × 167 mm.

handwritten originals were developed into typefaces, which retained some qualities of the handwritten form, including a degree of informality.

A second and more long-standing consequence of the print script movement was the use of sanserif typefaces in reading books. Some teachers thought that sanserif typefaces were similar to print script and thought it would be helpful to beginner readers to make a link. Nellie Dale had implied a connection when she made a link between 'printing' on the blackboard and on slates, and the sanserif letters used in the early volumes in her eponymous reading series published in 1899 (**19**). Fred Schonell made a similar point 50 years later:

> In the first introduction to a printed book the lines should
> be short, the type should not be less that 18 point and

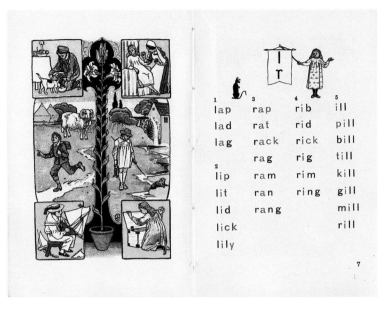

19 Detail from Nellie Dale, *On the teaching of English reading with a running commentary on the Walter Crane readers*, London: J.M. Dent, 1898, plate 9 and spread from 'The Dale readers', *Steps to reading*, London: George Philip & Sons, 1899, pp. 6–7. Page 181×122 mm.

The teacher Nellie Dale associated 'printed forms' (shown on the left in the handwritten examples) and sanserif type in her series of reading books.

should resemble as nearly as possible the print script that the child is acquainted with in his writing. This can be achieved by use of an 18 point Gil [sic] Sans type.[38] The availability of Monotype Gill Sans in 1928 and Stephenson Blake Granby in 1930 meant that there were alternatives to the late nineteenth-century grotesque typefaces that could be used for continuous text in reading books from the 1930s. Indeed, Beatrice Warde welcomed Gill Sans as a choice of 'major importance' for books for young children who 'see essentials to the exclusion of accidentals' – referring to the irrelevance of serifs for beginner readers.[39] Most support for sanserif forms, however, came from teachers and educationists and their views influenced publishers such that by the 1960s sanserif types were typically used: even reading schemes that had used serif typefaces produced 'print script' editions (see the example from 'The Janet and John books' on p. 77).

Single-storey a's and g's are integral to handwriting models and one of the ways that letterforms for reading and for writing could be aligned was by introducing alternative forms, or 'infant characters' as they became known, to the character set of

38. Fred Schonell, *The psychology and teaching of reading*, London: Oliver & Boyd, 1945, p. 20.

39. Warde, 'Annual or perennial', 1934, p. 15. Writing 20 years later Warde strongly promotes serifs as helpful in discriminating between similar letterforms, such as capital 'I' and lower-case 'el' (forms which in Gill Sans along with figure '1' are identical). Beatrice Warde, 'Improving the compulsory

book', *The Penrose Annual*, 1950, pp. 37–40. Warde was influenced by the work of Cyril Burt, especially his claim that serifs increased legibility. From 1954 they were frequent correspondents and Warde saw Burt's work as providing scientific validity to the views that she (and Stanley Morison) had promoted since the 1920s. Burt's work in relation to typography in school-books is

summarised in Watts & Nisbet, *Legibility in children's books*, 1974. For a detailed critique of Burt's legibility research see Ole Lund, 'Knowledge construction in typography: the case of legibility research and the legibility of sans serif typefaces', 1999, unpublished PhD thesis, Department of Typography & Graphic Communication, University of Reading.

Book design for children's reading

typefaces, whether serif or sanserif, used in reading books. An early example, shown in Figure **20**, was the single storey 'a' and 'g' used in 'The songs the letters sing', where the modified forms stand out due to inconsistency in line weight. Some infant characters were specially drawn by type designers: according to a teacher, Augusta Monteith, Eric Gill produced infant characters for Gill Sans at her request (**21**). The availability of infant characters and the promotion of Gill Sans as supporting the teaching of handwriting meant that from the 1930s it was a popular choice of typeface. Stephenson Blake's Granby, which shared characteristics of Gill Sans, was designed with a double storey 'a' and a single storey 'g', and was favoured by the publisher Schofield and Sims in, for example, 'The John and Mary readers' shown in Figure **22**. Some publishers responded to demand for infant characters by inserting sanserif single-storey a's and g's into serif text as in Figure **23**.

Though 'a' and 'g' were the most usually modified letters, from the 1960s onwards other infant characters were introduced, for example in Monotype Gill Sans, the 'l' and the 'J' and the number '4'. In the case of the 'l' a flick at the foot helped to distinguish it from the capital 'I' and figure '1'; the modification of the capital 'J' meant that it did not drop below the baseline; the figure '4' with an open top, was based on the handwritten forms that children would have been familiar with.[40] Some examples of typically modified characters are shown in Figure **24**. The use of Gill Sans with infant characters continued until the 1970s when its usage was superseded by versions of Helvetica, Univers, Frutiger, and Avant Garde Gothic which had very round a's and g's with very short descenders, resulting in letters that looked similar and that could be confusing for beginner readers.[41] By the 1980s infant characters were used in most reading schemes, even those that used serif typefaces. Indeed the use of infant characters was one of the features that distinguished

40. Awareness of different versions of the same letter may have been heightened by the Bullock Report (1975) which drew attention to the 'typographical variations' that occur within certain letters (beyond the capital/small letter distinction). The Report also highlighted the issue of different letter shapes within the context of a word, and the problems that children may encounter with this. That the Report also reinforced the relationship between a child's own handwriting with the development of their reading skills is likely to have further influenced – in the 1970s and 1980s – the use of infant characters. *Language for life*, section 6.10, pp. 81–2 [accessed through D. Gillard, *Education in England: a brief history*, 2011, www. educationengland.org.uk/history].

41. Some examples and further discussion of this can be found in Sue Walker and Linda Reynolds, 'Serifs, sans serifs and infant characters in children's reading books', *Information Design Journal + Document Design*, vol. 11, no. 2/3, 2002/3, pp. 106–22.

20 Detail from S. N. D. [Rose Meeres] 'The songs the letters sing', *Book IIA*, London and Glasgow: Grant Educational Company, *c*.1920, p. 38.

This unusual Edwardian jobbing typeface included specially drawn infant characters 'a' and 'g'.

> 2. When it is very cold the lambs have to be brought in or they would die. Mary's lamb must have grown up in

21 Detail from Augusta Monteith, *The pink book of verse*, London: Sheed & Ward, 1931, p. 10.

Cursive forms of 'a' and 'g' in Gill Sans from the book for which they were originally drawn. Monteith commented in a footnote: 'The type used throughout is the Sans-Serif of Mr. Eric Gill, who has designed cursive forms of 'a' and 'g' specially for this book.' p. vi.

> And a red nose;
> The longer she stands
> The shorter she grows.

22 Detail from Ellen Ashley 'The John and Mary readers', *Book four*, Huddersfield: Schofield & Sims, [1932–], p. 49.

The typeface, Granby, was also used for some of the 'Mac and Tosh' books from the same publisher.

> "So am I," said John.
> "It's moving," said Mary.
> "So it is," said John.

23 Detail from Harriett Carnell, 'Betty's geography lessons'. *Oranges and lemons*, London: George Gill & Sons, [1935], p. [2].

Gill Sans 'a' and 'g' have been substituted for the non-infant forms that would have been standard in the serif typeface.

> "Once a year," said Mother, "the children are given oranges and lemons

24 Detail from a type specimen produced by Oxprint *c*.1990 showing in red the infant character modifications made for their typeface Infantura, based on Futura.

> a b c d e f g h i j
> k l m n o p q r s
> t u v w x y z 1 2
> 3 4 5 6 7 8 9 0 ?

Book design for children's reading

books published by educational publishers from those produced by mainstream trade ones. Many teachers at this time supported the use of infant characters as found in a survey of teachers' opinions undertaken by Bridie Raban in the mid-1980s.[42]

An alternative view, and one that was put forward by Beatrice Warde in the 1930s, was that reading and writing were different activities and that non-infant characters, through their different form, could help distinguish between similar-looking characters:

> it seems a pity to familiarise them [children] with a and g of a form they will not meet in normal roman, and in the case of a, in a form which is more coincident with o and e than the unmistakable lower-case a'.[43]

In the 1990s in many British primary schools children were encouraged to choose books produced by educational and trade publishers according to a colour-coded scheme[44] which meant that beginner readers had the opportunity to encounter typefaces that had not been adapted for educational use, along with those that had, including forms of 'a' and 'g'.[45] Many trade publishers of books for young children combined serif typefaces with excellent use of space, as well as distinctive illustrations: Walker Books is an example of such a publisher whose books were used in schools that adopted an individualised reading approach and where seriffed typefaces without infant characters were nearly always used.

Using sanserif and serif typefaces to denote progression and reading levels

Different kinds of letterform were used in some cases to indicate progression from one reading stage to another. In 'The "Seandar" individual reading books', for example, the first two books in the series were handwritten, and the third one was set

42. Bridie Raban, 'Survey of teachers' opinions: children's books and handwriting styles'. In D. Dennis (ed.) *Reading: meeting children's special needs*, London: Heinemann, 1984, pp. 123–9.
43. Warde 'Annual or perennial', 1934, p. 15.
44. See for example, Cliff Moon, *Individualised reading*, Reading: Reading and Language Information Centre. This approach categorised books by readability according to colour-coded levels of difficulty. Published until 2007.

45. Sue Walker and Linda Reynolds found in classroom studies that many of the six-year-old children they talked with recognised there were two kinds of 'a' – one for reading and one for writing. Walker and Reynolds, 'Serifs, sans serifs and infant characters in children's reading books', 2002/3, p. 109. See also Vera Coghill, 'Can children read familiar words set in unfamiliar type'. *Information Design Journal*, vol. 1, no. 4, 1980, p. 260.

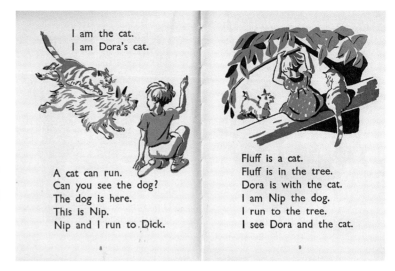

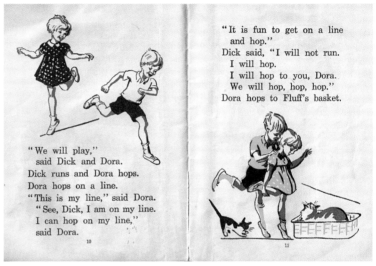

in Gill Sans. This practice was also followed in the 'Oxford reading tree' (1986) which used handwriting 'to simulate the writing done by the teacher' until Stage 4 when a version of Gill 'specially designed for the purpose, with educational a's and g's' was used.[46] Other series changed from a sanserif to a serif form in the later stages. 'The happy venture readers' was one of the first series to use a sanserif typeface for the initial books followed by a serif form for the later stages (**25**). The 'Ladybird key words reading scheme' in the 1960s showed progression through four different kinds of letterforms as well as a decrease in type size (**26**). The 'Puddle Lane' reading programme devised by Sheila McCullagh and published by Ladybird in the 1980s used serif and sanserif typefaces to denote different levels of reading. The text on the left-hand pages of the spread was set in Baskerville

46. Roderick Hunt, *Oxford reading
tree. Teacher's guide 1*, London: Oxford
University Press, 1986, p. 7.

Book design for children's reading

26 Pages from William Murray 'Ladybird key words reading scheme', Loughborough: Ladybird Books, 1960s (top left) *Book 2b Have a go*, 1964; (top right) *Book 3a Things we like*, 1964; (bottom left) *Book 7b Fun and games*, 1966; (bottom right) *Book 10a Adventure on the island*, 1966. Pages 171×112 mm.

The 'Ladybird key words reading scheme' used four typefaces according to the level of difficulty of the text. A 'handwritten' form was used for stages 1 and 2; Gill Sans for 3, 4, 5 and 6; a slab serif similar to Century Schoolbook for stages 7, 8 and 9; and Times New Roman for stages 10, 11 and 12. Using so many typefaces in one series was unusual as was, by the 1960s, justifying the text so that the word spaces varied. Particularly in the more advanced books the line spacing often varied from page to page, another practice likely to have been unhelpful to children. It is an example of a typesetting convention (vertical justification) over-riding the editorial solution of cutting the text so that each page had the same number of lines.

12·

I like Jane.

You like Jane.

We like Jane.

20

Here is the shop.

Peter and Jane look at
                    the dogs.
They look at the rabbits.

Look at this one,
              says Peter.
This is the one we want.

Yes, this is the one.

We want this rabbit.

new words

rabbits   one

10

Peter and Jane have a happy time on their holiday, away at the sea. Here they are at play on the sands. Aunty and Uncle are not with them this afternoon.

The two children run along the sands to fly their kite. First Peter has the kite and then Jane has a go with it. The brother and the sister let some of the other children play with them.

Then Peter lets the kite go out of his hand.

"Look," calls Jane, "it is going out to sea."

Peter says, "The kite is not going up any more. It will come down now. It will come down in the sea."

"We will make another one," says Jane.

"No," says Peter, "we may get this one back. We have a friend who could get our kite out of the sea for us. Let us go to find our friend to tell him about this."

8

As the children come back from the water they see their two cousins get out of a small car. It is their mother's car and she lets them drive it because they both drive very well.

The names of the two big boys are John and Simon. Peter and Jane and their father are happy to see them again. They all talk together for a while and then Father drives home by himself. He knows that John and Simon will look after Peter and Jane and not let them get into danger.

John and Simon pull a small boat down to the water's edge and tell Jane and Peter to get into it. Then the two big boys push the boat into the water and climb in.

John rows the small boat and, as he rows, his brother Simon talks to Peter and Jane. He says, " We are going to row out to our motor boat. It isn't a very large boat but it will take us to the island."

Jane says, " Isn't it fun ! Do we take the little boat with us ?"

" Yes," says Simon. " We pull it along behind the motor boat."

27 Spread from Sheila McCullagh, 'Puddle Lane', *When the magic stopped*, Loughborough: Ladybird Books, 1985, pp. 18–19. Page 170 × 112 mm.

The text on the left-hand pages of the spread were set in Baskerville for reading aloud and for fluent readers. On the right-hand page a smaller amount of text, set in Helvetica, was intended to be read by children.

"It's a wonderful saucer!" cried Tim.
He was very excited.
"Can you make it fly any faster?"

"I'll try," said Tessa.
She put her paw on the button.
"I wish to fly fast," she said.

The saucer flew faster and faster.
It flew over the river, and
over the hills.

The saucer flew
faster and faster.

18   19

and intended to be read aloud to the child by fluent readers. On the right-hand page a smaller amount of text, set in Helvetica, was intended to be read by children (**27**).

Special typefaces

Some typefaces have been specially designed to support children's reading needs. The Initial Teaching Alphabet (i. t. a.) was first used in some schools in the 1960s. Known by printers and publishers as 'Pitman's Augmented Alphabet', the i. t. a. was devised by Sir James Pitman. It was an 'augmented' roman alphabet in that additional characters were added that related to the principle sounds in English, such as long and short vowels and common digraphs (th, sh, ch). Pitman's intention was that the resulting 44-character alphabet would be used for the first two years of a child's time at school after which there would be transition to traditional orthography. Monotype produced a special typeface, 'Pitman i. t. a.', which was based on Erhardt and included modification of some existing characters and some new letterforms.[47] Unusually there were no capital letters, rather the capital letter function was fulfilled by larger versions of the small-letter shapes (**28**).

The i. t. a. was tested in schools to judge its effectiveness in improving the standards of reading. The experiment was undertaken with 41 classes of beginner readers being taught with the 'Janet and John' scheme using the i. t. a. and 41 classes being

47. The typeface in 12 point was made available free of copyright.

28 Detail from James Fassett, 'The Beacon readers', *Book 1, part 2: At play*, London: Ginn & Company, 1965 (first i.t.a. edition), p. 26.

jon   ie didn't see the big dog.

hou pritty fhee iz!

whot can wee doo with her?

father   muther will tell us whot too doo.

run and fiend her, jon.

rooth   tell her that father

has found a muther dog

and her littl bæby.

muther will bee good too them.

taught with the scheme in traditional orthography.[48] It was an ambitious project; both the phonic and look-and-say books in the Janet and John scheme were transliterated for the task.

The results of the initial experiment were positive, and the project was extended so that by 1966 the i.t.a. was used in many schools. According to an article in the *Monotype Recorder*, 'from 21 different publishing houses some two hundred different books for young readers have been transcribed into the new alphabet, and of these no fewer than 160 will be in print and in actual use by the time you read these words'.[49] Among these books were the 'Downing readers' and the 'Clearway readers' published by the Initial Teaching Publishing Company. Other educational publishers issued transliterations of existing series, such as the 'Beacon readers' (Ginn), 'Through the rainbow' (Schofield and Sims), 'Our book corner' (Chambers), 'Stories around us' (Longman) and 'The gay colour books' (E.J. Arnold) (**29–30**). The Ladybird 'Learning to read' series introduced a hand-produced version of the i.t.a. for the early stage books (**31**); more advanced ones were set in a much-enlarged version of the Monotype face.

48. The experiment was summarised in John Downing, 'Reform of the English writing system', *The Penrose Annual*, 1968, vol. 61, pp. 102–6; and is reported in detail in John Downing, *The i.t.a. reading experiment: three lectures on the research in infant schools with Sir James Pitman's Initial Teaching Alphabet*, London: Evans, 1964 and John Downing, *The i.t.a. symposium: research report on the British experiment with i.t.a.*, Slough: NFER, 1967.

49. 'Progress in P. A. A.', *The Monotype Recorder*, vol. 42, no. 3, 1962–3, p. 19.

29 Spread from James Fassett, 'The Beacon readers', *Book 1, part 2: At play*, London: Ginn & Company, 1965 (first i. t. a. edition), pp. 26–7. Page 202×134 mm. [DTC]

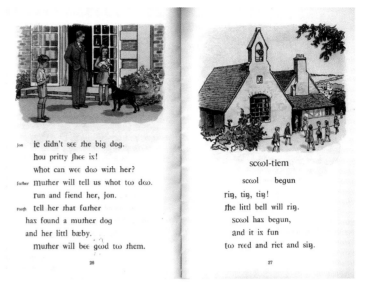

30 Spread from E. S. Bradburne, 'Through the rainbow', *Red book 1*, Huddersfield: Schofield and Sims Ltd, 1964, pp. 16–17. Page 247×182 mm. [DTC]

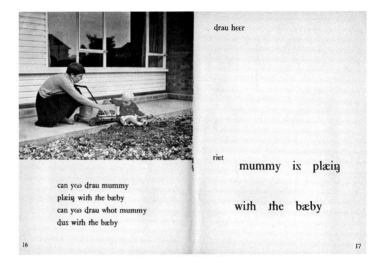

50. See Sir James Pitman, 'Learning to read with the augmented roman alphabet', *The Penrose Annual*, vol. 56, 1962, pp. 54–8; John Downing, 'Reform of the English writing-system', *The Penrose Annual*, vol. 61, 1968, pp. 102–5. *The Monotype Recorder*, vol. 42, no. 3, 1962–3, published to coincide with the anniversary of the birth of Sir Isaac Pitman, contained articles, 'Augmenting the Roman alphabet' by David Abercrombie, and 'Progress in P. A. A.' [Pitman's Augmented Alphabet] which was unacknowledged. A more recent account is Jeremy Hall, 'The Initial Teaching Alphabet', *Eye* 55, vol. 14, 2005, pp. 76–7.

The i. t. a. experiment certainly aroused interest in teachers, educationists and printers; it was also a typographic and publishing experiment and for this reason was reported in printing and publishing journals, much as had been the case with the newly cut Monotype faces in the 1920s and 1930s.[50] By the end of the 1960s, though, the i. t. a. had fallen out of favour because some children found it difficult to progress to traditional orthography, and teachers found they had to teach two systems in the classroom.

Another specially designed typeface was Sassoon Primary, produced in the 1980s after classroom research through which Rosemary Sassoon identified qualities that children preferred, such as lack of serifs and slight slant. The resulting typeface reflected these preferences, and though it had no serifs some of

31 Spread from Margaret Élise Gagg, 'A Ladybird learning to read book', *Numbers*, Loughborough: Wills and Hepworth, 1961, pp. 28–9. Page 171×112 mm. [DTC]

32 Detail from Rosemary Sassoon and Adrian Williams, *Why Sassoon?*, Publicity leaflet, 2000, pp. [2–3].

Exit strokes clump letters together.
These friendly letters were
researched with children

ÆŒABCDEFGHIJKLMNOPQRSTUVWXYZ&
æœabcdeffififlghiijklmnopqrstuvwxyzß
1234567890£$ƒ¢¥%*¶·/
.,:;!?''""„()[]/--—_«»‹›

the letters had 'exit strokes' which gave the type an informal and friendly 'feel'.[51] Single-storey a's and g's were integral to the font (**32**). Despite its child-centredness, Sasoon Primary had relatively little use as continuous text in reading schemes, and tended to be used in non-fiction books, such as the 'New horizons' science books published by Cambridge University Press in 1991, and for workbooks and other materials that supported reading schemes. It and its many variants were widely used in books for teaching handwriting.

In the 1980s and 1990s several publishers produced their own versions of typefaces, often with infant characters. With the use of desktop publishing, demand for typefaces suitable for children increased and specialist versions of a number of typefaces were produced by companies such as Oxprint, used by Oxford University Press. Heinemann's in-house design team produced

51. Rosemary Sassoon, 'Through the eyes of a child: perception and type design' in Rosemary Sassoon (ed.), *Computers and typography*, Oxford: Intellect Books, 1993, pp. 150–77. Sassoon Primary was the first in the Sassoon family of typefaces, which includes Sassoon Infant, Sasoon Joiner and many others (see www.sassoonfont.co.uk).

33 Example of Heinemann roman (source: http://origin.myfonts.com/s/aw/original/91/0/46834.pdf).

its own font for its early primary materials. Released in 2008, this typeface, Heinemann, was developed in collaboration with children, literacy advisors and teachers, and was trialled in schools over eight years (**33**).

Widely-used typefaces

From the 1920s until the end of the 1970s Gill Sans was a popular choice for books for younger readers. Regarded by teachers as suitable because of its clarity, simplicity and perceived similarity to handwriting, it was also a typeface that was readily available. As well as incorporating infant 'a' and 'g' from an early stage, it was also available in bold and light variants, both of which were used occasionally in reading books as seen in Figure **34**. Gill was also used in non-educational children's books of one kind or another, such as 'The youngest readers' series published by Nelson in the 1930s, and this helped to reinforce its child-friendly associations (**35**). A second widely-used typeface was Century Schoolbook, first introduced by Ginn in its 'Beacon' readers in the 1920s. Century, unlike Gill Sans, had no association with handwriting. Its clear appearance was due to its relatively heavy weight, open counters and generous lateral space. But another reason for the success of Century as a reading book typeface was the way in which it was used. Series of reading books that were imported to the UK from the USA, such as the 'Beacon' and 'Field' readers, displayed generous space between lines and words, and ranged-left setting. Such visual attributes contributed to book pages that were legible and accessible

34 Spreads from 'Evans activity readers', *Out to play*, London: Evans, [1947], pp. 18–19 (top) and 'The Kathy and Mark basic readers', *Kathy and Mark*, London: James Nisbet, 1970, pp. 14–15. Page 210 × 150 mm.

Gill Sans in bold and light variants was occasionally used in reading books.

35 Detail from 'The youngest readers', *Toy tales*, London: Thomas Nelson and Sons, [1939], pp. [22–3]. Reproduced actual size.

Gill was widely available due in part to its popularity for non-educational children's books as in this example from a series of large format story books set in 36 point.

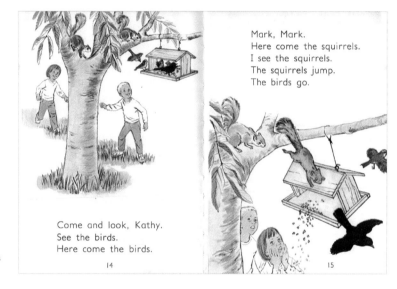

> "Wait a minute," said Ann, "I'm going to fetch something." She ran into the house and brought out a lovely new skipping rope. It was white with wooden handles of red and blue.
> "Watch me," she said, "I can skip."
> "One, two, three, four!" She went on skipping to twenty-one without stopping.

Mark, Mark.
Here come the squirrels.
I see the squirrels.
The squirrels jump.
The birds go.

Come and look, Kathy.
See the birds.
Here come the birds.

14

15

Nanny had a tiny silver
It had been given to
when she was a little girl,

36 Spread from Walter Taylor Field, 'The Field readers', *Book two*, London: Ginn and Company, [1927], pp. 20–21. Page 183 × 135 mm.

Century Schoolbook, with generous spacing, was used in several series published by Ginn.

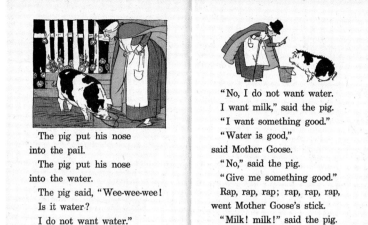

The pig put his nose
into the pail.
The pig put his nose
into the water.
The pig said, "Wee-wee-wee!
Is it water?
I do not want water."
20

"No, I do not want water.
I want milk," said the pig.
"I want something good."
"Water is good,"
said Mother Goose.
"No," said the pig.
"Give me something good."
Rap, rap, rap; rap, rap, rap,
went Mother Goose's stick.
"Milk! milk!" said the pig.
21

(Figure **36**). The success of the 'Janet and John' books from 1949 further reinforced the appeal of Century Schoolbook.

Use of space and typographic variation

Choice of typeface, as has been discussed, was influenced by the views of different groups of people: teachers, legibility researchers, printers, publishers and publicists. There has been less intervention about the use of horizontal and vertical space and the overall layout of text on a page, which continued to be influenced by compositors and those who prepared pages for printing and resulted in justified setting being used in most reading books until around the mid 1940s.

From around the 1920s, however, some books were set ranged left with even word spacing, or gave the appearance of being ranged left (**37**). A significant influence on the adoption of ranged-left setting and even word spacing was the pedagogic imperative to relate line-breaks to the sense of the text[52] as in 'The new beacon readers' (1922–1930) referred to by Morss in his 'Neglected schoolbook' article in 1934, in a caption to a page from *Book 2:*

> One of the most difficult problems in building the infants' first book is to ensure that each line and each turnover corresponds with the reading matter.[53]

52. The issues of exactly where lines should be broken in accordance with sense was explored by Bridie Raban in the 1980s. She concluded that the problems of where to break the line in texts for beginner readers was not straightforward. The most significant finding of her research was that 'and' should not occur at the beginning of a line; its location at the end of a line anticipated the text that followed. Bridie Raban, 'Text display effects on the fluency of young readers', *Journal of Reading Research*, vol. 5, no. 1, 1982, pp. 7–28.

53. p. [5].

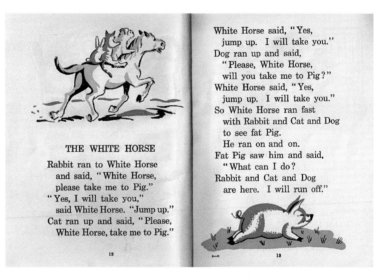

54. Fred Schonell, *The happy venture teacher's manual*, Edinburgh: Oliver and Boyd, 1959, p. 28. Schonell had first discussed this, showing examples from the 'Happy venture' scheme, in *The psychology and teaching of reading*, 1945.

Fred Schonell in *The teacher's manual* for 'The happy venture readers', first published in 1959, expressed similar views very clearly:

> all-important is the printing of the material so that the amount in a line and the break of the lines fit with the mechanics of the reading process and with the understanding of the material to be read. In other words, we need to pay attention both to the 'eye span units' and the 'meaning units'.[54]

This approach was implemented in the books in 'The happy venture readers' (**38**).

Recognition of the potential significance of line endings in helping children learn to read, among other things, affirmed the growing influence of pedagogy on the visual appearance of reading books. Comments about typography began to appear in some of the teacher's manuals that accompanied some of the reading schemes. Ellen Ashley, in the *Teacher's book* for 'The John and Mary readers' [1932], for example, included comments on the quality of typography suitable for primers:

> Then in the actual printing of the primers, apart from the big print, good spacing, good margins, simple attractive illustrations, etc., there should be thought about the phrasing. Roughly, the lines should be arranged in phrases that can be seen at a glance, so that the child's eye will be trained from the first to move rhythmically.[55]

Exactly what she meant by 'big' in relation to type size and 'good' in relation to spacing can only be worked out by looking at relevant pages which shows that the type is well spaced. Fred Schonell also affirmed that adequate space between words and lines was important for beginner readers: 'It is not only the size of print that makes a difference, but the space between the letters, the words and the lines.'[56] *The Janet and John manual*, first published in 1954, related the use of space to other attributes that affected the 'look and feel' of the books in the scheme:

> In the Janet and John books the greatest care has been taken to produce books that are attractive and satisfying as books. Paper of high quality has been chosen because only on good paper can print be clear and black, as it must for children's eyes, and only on good paper can colours be reproduced as clearly and precisely as they should be. Ample space has been allowed for the reading matter, since over-crowding the page is another cause of eye-strain. The typeface chosen – Century – is notably clear, well-formed and free from affectation. It was designed by Bruce Rogers for use in school books, and all its letters except a and g have the same outline form as print script.[57]

The author's knowledge of typography was clearly somewhat shaky – Morris Fuller Benton designed Century Schoolbook, and because it was a serif typeface it did not have the same outline as 'print script'. It is nevertheless interesting that there is reference to 'ample space', something not usually referred to. Some examples of the 'good' and 'ample' spacing referred to in books for teachers that accompanied reading schemes are shown in Figure **39**.

55. Ellen Ashley, 'The John and Mary readers', *Teacher's book*, Huddersfield: Schofield and Sims, [1932], p.15.
56. Schonell, *The psychology and teaching of reading*, 1945, p.21.
57. Rona Munro, *A teachers' manual for use with the Janet and John reading course*, Welwyn: James Nisbet & Co., 1954, p.1.

Book design for children's reading

39 Spreads from Mabel O'Donnell and Rona Munro, 'Janet and John', *Book three*, Edinburgh and London: James Nisbet & Co, *c*.1950, pp. 66–7 and from Elspeth Ashley, 'The John and Mary readers', *John and Mary's painting day*, Huddersfield: Schofield and Sims, [1943], pp. [30–31]. Pages 198 × 138 mm and 130 × 102 mm.

Examples of typography from series where, in the teacher's manuals, reference is made to typography. In both cases short lines, generous line spacing and wide margins contribute to pages that are inviting to read.

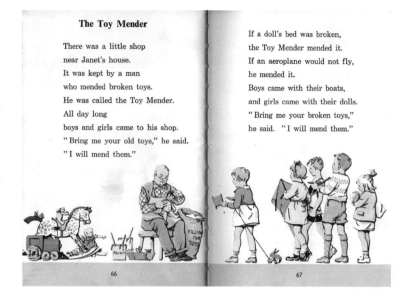

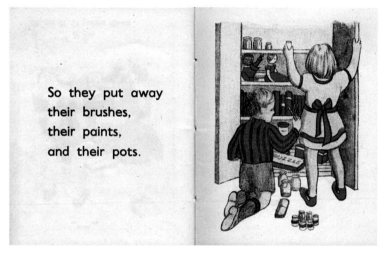

By the 1950s most reading books adhered to generous margins and adequate space between lines and words. During the 1960s, however, there were examples of unusual and rather extreme typography: very large type, excessive space between lines, very bold type and short lines (**40–41**). Such unconventional approaches did little to prepare the child for adult reading, but perhaps represented the child-centred and experimental approach to teaching that was promoted at the time. This was also seen in debate about when punctuation marks and capital letters should be introduced. A number of schemes published in the 1970s used neither. The *Yellow books* in the 'Breakthrough to literacy' scheme, for example, did not use any capital letters except 'I', and the only punctuation marks were full points, which resulted in some unusual configurations particularly when direct speech was represented (**42**).

40 Spread from Gertrude Cree, 'Getting ready to read', *The broken toys*, London: Frederick Warne, 1967, pp. [4–5]. Page 200 × 140 mm.

The space between the lines here is excessive and is likely to interrupt the flow of continuous reading.

Donald's kite

is broken.

"Grandad will fix it,"

said Donald.

41 Details from Vera Card, 'Let's read', *Book 2*, Edinburgh: Holmes McDougall, 1964, pp. 6–7 and from Cecilia and Jean Hinde, 'Corkey books', *Bad baby*, Edinburgh: Oliver & Boyd, 1960, showing the type reproduced actual size.

Two examples of the extreme typography used by some publishers in the 1960s.

See me walk

to the door.

Mummy is washing

my teddy bear's

clothes

Book design for children's reading

42 Spreads and detail from David Mackay, Brian Thompson and Pamela Schaub, 'Breakthrough to literacy', *things I can do* (top) and *after school*, London: Longman, 1970. Pages 184 × 124 mm.

'Breakthrough' was one of the schemes that dropped capital letters apart from 'I' and punctuation marks apart from full points in the early books in the scheme. The disadvantages of this approach are seen in the bottom spread where the addition of appropriate punctuation would have helped to articulate the meaning of the text.

we can make things.

I paint a picture.

6

7

children time for bed says mum.

oh no say the children.

10

11

goodnight says mum.
goodnight says dad.

43 Spread from 'Royal school series', *The royal crown infant reader*, London: Thomas Nelson, nd (reprinted until at least 1945), pp. 22–3. Page 182 × 121 mm.

A sanserif typeface used for a word list.

22	INFANT READER.

has to do. On he runs, till he comes to the baker's shop. Dan goes in, and puts down his basket, and then gives a bark.

4. The baker lifts the lid, and takes out the penny. Then Dan barks again, and wags his tail. He knows all about it.

5. Into the basket the baker puts two rolls. Then Dan wags his tail again. That is his way of saying "Thank you." Then Dan lifts his basket, and runs off home.

6. He does not stop to play on the way. And he does not lay down his basket, till he gets to his master's door.

7. His master pats him, and says, "Good dog, good Dan!" Then Dan is very happy.

INFANT READER.   23

9. MAY'S BIRTH-DAY.

birth	reads	shy
years	string	milk
feels	start	jumps
says	kit-ty	nurse

1. It is May's birth-day. She is six years old. She feels far too big to play with dolls.

2. But what is this she sees on the rug? It is a round basket, with a paper tied to it.

Differentiation through typographic variation

Since the nineteenth century, variation in typeface, weight and colour has been used to differentiate elements within a page or spread. In many early twentieth-century reading books, sanserif typefaces were used for spelling exercises, headings, emphasis or for articulating particular elements of a narrative (**43**). A list of new words at the start of a reading lesson or page was a characteristic feature in many books, and was differentiated from the main text by changing the typeface, by increasing the type size, by using a bolder weight, by underlining, or by combining these (**44**). Punctuation marks and other typographic devices were used in some cases to denote syllables as 'rib-bon', 'sleep-ing'; or to encourage the 'sounding out' of a word as 'b-at', 'm-uch'. Vertical and horizontal rules were sometimes used as decoration, or to aid direction of reading.

The use of a typeface bolder than that used for the main text for lists of new words was a typical feature of many nineteenth-century reading books. One of the earliest series that offered an explanation was 'The Midland readers' (Simpkin, Marshall & Co, 1873), which used bold type for lists of new words, and also when they appeared in the text. This was regarded as 'a new and curious method' by a contemporary review[58] not least because this was explained to the young readers:

Do you want to know why I have put the hard words at the top of the page?

58. 'The Midland readers', *The School Board Chronicle*, 1 November 1873, p. 430.

44 Examples of typographic treatments for wordlists from a selection of late nineteenth- and early twentieth-century reading books.

voice   laugh   opened   poor

| a-live′ | teach | rib′bon | flies |
| a-wake′ | learn | sleep′ing | stripes |

im · am · an
r..im : ram : can
J..im : jam : ron
h..im : ham : man

im
am
an

N n
Nan

ink   ank   unk   imp   emp

wink	bank	bunk	limp	hemp
pink	tank	sunk	crimp	
sink	sank	trunk		
think	thank			
drink	drank			
rink	prank			

1. New Words.

rain	pat′ter	locked	noth′ing
pray	play′things	bricks	else
pit′ter	broke	naugh′ty	win′dow

sash	dish
hush	fish
rush	wish

l-eft	l-oft	s-uch
g-ift	s-oft	m-uch
l-ift	t-uft	r-ich

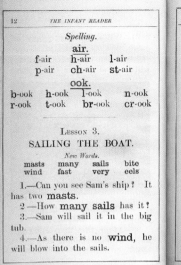

I want you to learn these off by heart, so that when you read the book you will not have to stop and spell out the words …

And do you see I have also put the hard words in the lines in nice bold print, so that your eye may be fixed on them, and then you will know then again when you see them.[59]

'Longmans' new readers' (1891) was another series where key words were highlighted in the text by increasing the size, as well as typeface and weight (**45**). Such articulation within the text was rare beyond the end of the nineteenth century. In most cases the words were presented conventionally as continuous text with little variation in letterforms. In the 1980s some educational publishers began to enliven their pages with expressive typography, or by using speech bubbles for the main text (**46**). Occasionally the way the words were organised spatially echoed the meaning of the text, as in the example in 'The romance of reading' shown in Figure **47**.

59. H. Major, 'The Midland Readers', *Book I*, London: Simpkin Marshall & Co, 1870s, p.3. The use of bold type for key words in a reading book was unusual at the time, though the use of bold or bold-looking types to distinguish parts of a text from another was widely used in timetables, dictionaries, directories and catalogues from the 1840s and 1850s. This practice became a characteristic feature in school textbooks, and in some reading books in the last quarter of the nineteenth century and beyond. Michael Twyman drew attention to what he called 'variegated typography' in 'The bold idea: the use of bold-looking types in the nineteenth century', *Journal of the Printing Historical Society*, vol. 22, 1993, pp.107–43.

Book design for children's reading

46 Spreads from Pat Edwards, 'Longman reading world', *Greedy pigs*, Harlow: Longman, 1987, pp. 10–11. Illustrated by Maggie Ling (top) and from Joyce Zemke, 'Journeys through reading', *Supper for a troll*, Huddersfield: Schofield & Sims, 1984, p. 7. Illustrated by June Lawrason. Pages 240 × 185 mm and 232 × 183 mm. [DTC]

In these examples a variety of letterform styles and typographic treatments reflects the meaning of the words.

47 Spread from Hilda Haig-Brown and Zillah Walthew, 'The romance of reading infant series', *Playbook 1*, London: Oxford University Press, 1943, pp. 14–15. Illustrated by Marcia Lane Foster. Page 189 × 145 mm.

Type and image are closely related in books in this series.

48 Spreads from James Webster, 'Rescue reading', *Martin the mouse*, London: Ginn and Co, 1968, p. 47 (top); Jessie Mackinder, 'The Chelsea readers', *Book 2*, London: Harrap, 1946, p. 34–5 (middle); and Hilda Haig Brown and Zillah Walthew, 'The romance of reading infant series', *Book 2, At the shops*, Oxford: Oxford University Press, pp. 28–9. Pages 210 × 144 mm; 215 × 140 mm and 189 × 145 mm.

Examples of the use of a second colour in text.

"If you do not land
I will shoot."
We will crash,
thought my Dad.
I have got to get
that gun.
But how?
The second pilot put
the wheels down.

46

Then he sniffed.
"Something is burning,"
he said.
My Dad looked down.
Smoke was coming from
the radio.
"We are on fire!"
he shouted.

47

34

sh   wish
ship fish
      shut

Daddy put a shelf up in the shed.
Fred put his ship and his shrimp net on the shelf in the shed.
Fanny said, "I wish I had a shelf in the shed."

Lesson 24

35

Daddy said, "You shall have a shelf."

"I shall put it by Fred's shelf."

Fanny said, "If I can I shall get shells to put on my shelf.

Pink shells are very pretty.

Lesson 24 *(continued)*

I put my pennies in a box when Father gives them me.
One day I'll get my pennies out
to buy a Christmas tree.

put, buy, Father,   day

28

Mother says, "We must not forget to buy some hay for the hens."
Pat and Ted have some hens, you see.
Father puts a little nest of hay for the mother hen, and she lays her eggs on it.

29

Use of colour in text

Colour was used occasionally to differentiate letters, words, or larger sections of text in reading books. It was used for headings, to draw attention to particular letter combinations, to reinforce or supplement methods of teaching reading by using red to highlight rhymes to be learnt by children to reinforce the sentence method of teaching, and to denote particular parts of text such as direct speech (**48**).[60]

At the end of the nineteenth century Nellie Dale's scheme introduced colour to represent letter sounds, but though the 'Dale readers' were popular and used in schools for many years, it was not until the progressive, informal and child-centred 1960s that new ideas using colour as part of a teaching method emerged.[61] Many of such developments were led by practising teachers and were reflected in the visual organisation of reading books.[62] There were, for example, a number of approaches that introduced colour as a way of distinguishing between different sounds. In the 'Words in colour' approach to teaching reading, devised by Gattegno, children were taught to associate particular colours with particular sounds – regardless of how they were spelt, and teachers used coloured chalks on the blackboard to explain this.[63] The reading books used to support the scheme, however, were printed in black and white in curious configurations that related to what children would have been doing in the classroom. 'Colour-story reading' was another complicated scheme that was supported by the Department of Education and Science who funded research and development at the Reading Research Unit, University of London (also involved in the i. t. a. testing). This scheme used colour and particular shapes to differentiate between sounds, shown with an explanation in Figure **49**. The 'Patterns of sound' scheme used a traffic light system to reinforce a method of teaching that resulted in some colourful reading books where red, orange and green were used to indicate 'stop', 'get ready' and 'go into' (**50**). The system was based around the idea that children should be taught to understand the relationship between the sounds of the written symbols of the alphabet and how the sounds are made with the mouth and breath.[64] 'Reading by rainbow' was another teacher-inspired scheme produced for reluctant readers. It used four colours: black for letters with 'their usual phonetic sound'; red for long vowel sounds; blue for 'd' (to distinguish it from 'b'), and for the 'oo' sound in 'too';

60. As noted by Watts and Nisbet in their review (1974, p. 74), the use of large amounts of coloured type may decrease legibility; they summarise Tinker's work on the legibility of coloured ink on white and coloured paper (see also, Miles Tinker, *Bases for effective reading*, Ames: Iowa State University Press, 1965).

61. Dale, *On the teaching of English reading*, 1898. Her scheme did not meet with universal approval, see for example, B. Dumville, 'The methods of teaching reading in the early stages', *The School World*, November 1912, p. 408 which criticised the phonic method and Dale's in particular.

62. For a summary account of some of these approaches, see Hugh Philip and Judith Goyen, 'Innovation in reading', *Experiments and innovations in education, no. 3*, Paris: UNESCO, 1973 and the three volumes of proceedings arising from the first, second and third international reading symposia, edited by John Downing and published by Cassell in 1966, 1967 and 1968.

63. A brief review of this scheme is Joan Dean, 'Words in colour', *The first international reading symposium*, ed. John Downing, London: Cassell, 1966, pp. 74–91. See also J. Kenneth Jones, 'Phonetic colour reading' in *The third international reading symposium*, ed. John Downing & Amy Brown, London: Cassell, 1968, pp. 91–106.

64. Gertrude Baldwin, *Patterns of sound: a book of alliterative verse. A method of learning to read successfully for beginners and reluctant readers*, London: The Chartwell Press, 1967.

49 Detail and page from J. Kenneth Jones, 'Colour story reading', *Teacher's manual*, London: Nelson, 1967. Page 222 × 165 mm. (top) illustration 1 and (bottom) illustration 3. [DTC]

This seemingly complicated scheme used colour and shape to differentiate sounds. In the top example the different sounds of 'cou' are represented in different graphic ways. The author claims: 'Colour not only assists decoding, it also encourages reading a word from left to right when working out the sounds. This is because each coloured letter and each colour symbol contains completely reliable phonetic information, which does not depend on the letters following'.

In the lower example, the illustration of the wall chart that accompanies the scheme shows its components: 35 coloured letters, 9 digraphs, and 9 coloured backgrounds. Each letter is allocated a colour and the colour only changes when the letter changes its sound or when letters form part of a digraph. Letters that children might find it difficult to distinguish between are listed vertically on the chart and differentiated by colour.

The nine differently-shaped coloured backgrounds represent different sounds, for example, a green circle represents the 'oo' sound; a blue triangle the 'sh' sound and a blue circle silent letters. The system is explained in the *Teacher's manual;* one of the rules of the system is that letters of similar shape should have different colours; another that there should be a similar number of symbols in each colour.

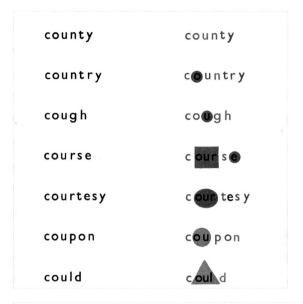

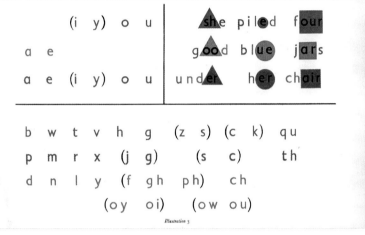

50 Pages from Gertrude Baldwin, 'Patterns of sound', London: The Chartwell Press, 1968. Page 247 × 183 mm. [DTC]

In this scheme orange, green and red are used to represent get ready, go into and stop.

Book design for children's reading

go, bob.
go to get a
  bone.
bob has got a
  bone.
see bob and
his big bone.

3

tom has a boat.
it is a big
  red boat.
the big red boat
  is on a pond.

the big red boat
can sail on a
  pond.

4

and yellow for letters that were not sounded. The resulting pages appeared rather disjointed with the black letters more prominent than the others (**51**). Despite considerable interest in colour schemes, the Bullock Report (1975) noted that only 6 per cent of classes were using them, and that findings about their value were inconclusive:

> The more elaborate schemes may be said to exact too high a price in terms of the amount of attention they demand and the consequent distraction from meaning. Simpler schemes which signal more general functions (e.g. silent letters, the grouping of letters), rather than specific sound values may well have something to offer, though this has yet to be convincingly demonstrated.[65]

65. *Language for life*, section 7.26, p. 109.

52 Nellie Dale, 'The Dale readers', *Second primer*, London: George Phillip & Son, *c*.1900. 181 × 122 mm.

The 'Dale readers' at the beginning of the nineteenth century was an early example of a scheme where the text and high quality illustrations were given equal prominence.

Pictures in books
for teaching reading

The timeline beginning on page 84 shows considerable variety both in style of illustrations and in their treatment. Line drawings, simple or detailed shaded drawings, and photographs which in turn may be squared-up or boxed, bled off on one or more edges, or integrated across a page, were used to illustrate the books, with colour added to the entire image, or to foreground or background elements. Using a particular named illustrator, or approach to illustrations for a series of books, was to become a characteristic feature of many graded reading schemes. Walter Crane produced a wealth of immediately recognisable large and small illustrations in full colour for 'The Dale readers' (**52**).[66] Margaret Tarrant, well-known for her fairy pictures, was chosen by the Grant Educational Company to illustrate 'The songs the letters sing' and subsequently 'Simple reading steps', both very popular series. Other distinctive illustrations included those developed by Rita Townsend for 'The Mac and Tosh readers'; by Florence and Margaret Hoopes for 'Janet and John'; and by Lilian Chivers with the 'The gay way' scheme. Specially commissioned and art-directed black-and-white photography was an unusual and distinctive illustrative mode for the 'Growing and reading' series published by Macmillan in 1956, and in the 1960s colour photographs were used in a number of schemes such as 'Dominoes' published by Oliver & Boyd and 'Through the rainbow' by Schofield & Sims. Particularly in books published in the 1980s and 1990s that contained more than one story, or reading schemes that comprised many individual titles (such as 'Breakthrough'), different illustrators contributed to considerable variation in style and approach.

One of the most noticeable visual characteristics of reading books over time is the increase in the use of coloured illustrations within a page or spread. This trend had origins in the nineteenth century when availability of cheap colour printing encouraged publishers to take advantage of it to promote and sell their books.[67] Collins was one of the first publishers to do this in the aptly named 'Graphic' series of readers and primers, part of 'Collins' school series' first published in 1891. 'With coloured

66. Nellie Dale evidently worked closely with Crane; he even visited her classroom: 'So great was the interest in the crab that when Mr Walter Crane visited us, special requests were made by the children for a sketch of it. The crab was immediately drawn in the attitude desired (a claw just peeping out of the cap) and submitted to their approval. It is needless to say that it met with the warmest reception.' Dale, *On the teaching of reading*, p. 34.

67. Michael Twyman, 'The illustration revolution' in David McKitterick (ed.) *The Cambridge history of the book in Britain, vol. VI 1830–1914*, Cambridge: Cambridge University Press, 2009, pp. 117–43 and *Printing 1770–1970: an illustrated history of its development and uses in England*, London: The British Library, 1998, (2nd edn).

53 Spread from 'Collins school series', *The graphic infant reader, no. 2*, London and Glasgow: Collins, *c.*1891, pp. 54–5. Page 176 × 120 mm.

Collins was a publisher quick to exploit colour printing at the end of the nineteenth century. 'With eight full-page coloured illustrations' appeared on the title page of *The graphic infant reader*.

68. See John Southward, *Modern printing: a handbook*, London: Raithby, Lawrence & Company, 1898, pp. 236–56 for a detailed explanation of imposition; and Hugh Williamson, *Methods of book design: the practice of an industrial craft*, London: Oxford University Press, 1966 (2nd edn), pp. 224–8.

illustrations' and 'high-class illustrations' were two phrases that appeared on the covers of the two primers in the series. The primers and readers used a black-and-white or coloured illustration to precede each lesson (**53**); and one innovative feature took advantage of the ability to print across the centre spread of the book to include a single large picture that ran across both pages in that position in each book. The updated 'New graphic readers' published in 1898 used an even larger variety of illustrations: full-page ones from colour photographs, black-and-white photographs, coloured engravings, black-and-white line engravings and black-and-white tone engravings. These appeared throughout the book presenting an image of a publisher who could see that exciting and colourful illustrations was one way to capture this particular market. The position of the coloured illustrations would have been influenced by the way the printers imposed the book pages for printing – one sheet would contain all the colour pictures and when it was folded and collated with black-only pages, the colour pages would be interspersed.[68] Many reading books produced in the early part of the twentieth century followed this practice, seen for example in the *First infant reader* in 'The Oxford reading books' series (*c.*1915) which had a full-colour frontispiece, and full- and half-page colour pictures on some of the pages throughout the book (**54**).

Some publishers continued to produce reading books with pictures in black and white only. This may have been for reasons of economy, and may also have been influenced by a view that

Book design for children's reading

54 Title-page and two spreads from ' The Oxford reading books', *Infant reader 1*, London: Oxford University Press, *c.*1915. Page 180 × 123 mm.

A full-colour, full-page title page was a typical feature of reading books from this period. Most, as here, had a caption and reference to the page of related text. Full-colour, full-page and half-page illustrations were used throughout the book on alternate spreads determined by the way that the pages were imposed for printing. Other illustrations were printed in black only.

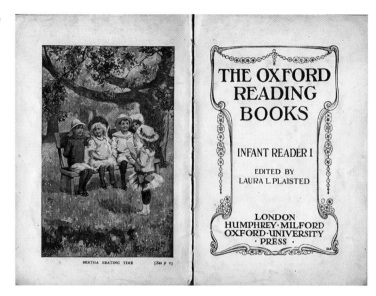

BERTHA BEATING TIME   [*See p* 23

THE OXFORD READING BOOKS

INFANT READER I

EDITED BY
LAURA L. PLAISTED

LONDON
HUMPHREY·MILFORD
OXFORD·UNIVERSITY
· PRESS ·

---

14   FIRST INFANT READER

" See, Hilda ! Kitty is running after her tail ! "

But Hilda laid her dolly by the side of the train, and ran into the kitchen to see Mother.

When Father came home to dinner the rain had quite stopped, so the children went with him to the gate.

LESSON 6.—*ay.*

EDDY AND MAY.

" Can Eddy come to-day, Mother?" asked Alfred.

" Yes," said Mother. " It is fine to-day. Ask him to bring May; she will like to play with Hilda."

Eddy is Alfred's play-mate, and May is his little sister.

So Alfred fetched Eddy and

FIRST INFANT READER   15

May, and the four children had a gay time.

Alfred's Father gave them a ride on Dapple, the gray mare. Then they had a game with Tray, the big black and white dog. He lay

---

28   FIRST INFANT READER

LESSON 12.—*ar.*

MR. MARSH, THE FARMER.

" Mr. Marsh has asked us to go and see his garden," said Mother. " We had better go on the car ; it is too far for Alfred's legs ! We will start at ten o'clock, and we can go to the market on the way home."

Mr. Marsh was a farmer. He had a charming garden, as well as a farm. Mother and the children were glad to go with him into the farmyard, and then to the garden.

" Come and see my orchard," he said. " You can pick up the apples and plums if you like, Alfy."

Then he gave Alfred and Hilda a ride in his cart, and at last Mother said they must go home.

A RIDE IN THE FARMER'S CART

55 Pages from Ellen Ashley, 'The John and Mary readers', *Book 3. John and Mary's Christmas party*, Huddersfield: Schofield & Sims, 1930s. Illustrated by E. L. Turner. Page 184 × 136 mm.

From the preface: 'The lino-cut pictures are a unique feature of the Series. They are of a similar type to wood engravings which were employed prior to the invention of photo-engraving … In the first instance these lino-cuts were prepared by Miss Turner as an experiment in connection with illustrative work in a few schools, but their newness and boldness provided so attractive to the children that it was thought that the pictures merited a wider public.'

coloured pictures were not necessary or beneficial in books for teaching reading. James Kerr wrote about this in 1926:

> Line illustrations are preferable to half-tone work both from visual and educational considerations. Black and white is the only kind necessary for ordinary school purposes.[69]

His final remark perhaps suggested that school-books were of second-order status, but may also have encouraged distinctive monochrome pictures such as the 'simple attractive illustrations' in the 'John and Mary readers' (1930s)[70] where striking black-and-white lino-cuts are used for the main books in the series (**55**).

By the 1960s the use of full-colour illustrations in reading books was widespread. Prior to this, to save on printing costs books were often printed with one or two spot colours, usually in addition to black, to create a colourful appearance.[71] A single solid colour would be used to add highlights to the illustrations, or broken down to add to tonal range. Careful use of two colours, in addition to black, resulted in a range of tones and overprints that provided considerable pictorial interest. The use of large blocks of solid colour, such as the red and green in the 'Mac and Tosh' series, and red and blue in *Playbook 1* of 'The romance of reading' resulted in bold, graphic images that became a distinctive feature (**56**). There are occasional examples of particularly economical use of colour where the text was printed in a dark colour other than black. In *The shy little sea horse*, the text was printed in dark green, which was then used in a range of tints to add pictorial interest (**57**).

69. James Kerr, *The fundamentals of school health*, London: Allen and Unwin, 1926, pp. 556–7.

70. Ashley, *Teacher's book*, 'John and Mary readers', p. 15.

71. Without large print runs the cost of full colour would have been prohibitive. Robert Morss referred to the average annual expenditure of 1s 7.9d per child on school books cited in the 1928 Hadow Report, and reflected that the publishers' reward 'on even the most successful school book will at best be comparatively modest.' He commented in a footnote that the Hadow Committee had estimated that the amount spent on books was less than 1 per cent of total expenditure on education in England and Wales. Morss, 'The neglected schoolbook', 1935, p. 4.

56 Spread from Ellen Ashley, *Mac and Tosh with Jim and Jenny*, Huddersfield: Schofield and Sims, 1930s, pp. 18–19. Illustrated by Rita Townsend. Page 184 × 138 mm.

Large blocks of solid colour (red and green on alternate spreads) are a characteristic feature of the 'Mac and Tosh' books.

57 Spread from Eileen Ryder, 'Stories for me', *The shy little sea horse*, London: Macmillan, 1959, pp. [2–3]. Illustrated by Esmé Jeudwine. Page 185 × 133 mm.

This example shows the use of dark green, rather than black, for the text. Tints of green are then used to good effect in the illustrations.

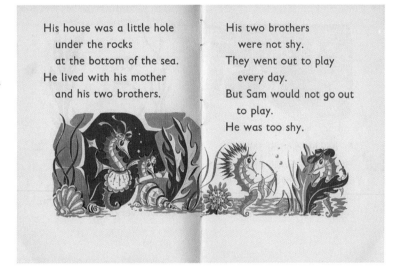

72. Evelyn Goldsmith, *Research into illustration: an approach and a review*, Cambridge: Cambridge University Press, 1984, in particular Chapter 2 'The place of illustrations in the teaching of reading'. A summary of Goldsmith's work, for illustrated books in general and for older infants, is 'Learning from illustrations: factors in the design of illustrated educational books for middle-school children', *Word and Image*, vol. 2, no. 2, April–June 1986, pp. 111–21.

The books represented in the timeline show that the trend through the twentieth century was towards colourful picture-dominated books that emphasised the perceived importance of illustrations in books for beginner readers. But are they helpful in the process of learning to read? A review by Evelyn Goldsmith surveyed research literature including experiments that had looked at the role and effectiveness of pictures in learning to read.[72] What emerged from this was that many studies, particularly those concerned with the acquisition of individual words, concluded that pictures were a distraction. Many experiments, however, used poor quality illustrations and test material, or had complicated, inconclusive results.

However, and more relevant here, the motivational reasons for using pictures in books for teaching reading have been articulated in teachers' manuals accompanying reading schemes since the 1930s.[73] The teachers' book to the 'John and Mary readers' (*c.*1932) discussed the importance of a 'reading atmosphere' that introduced children to words and pictures relevant to everyday things so that 'the children will naturally want to talk about the pictures'. And from 'The romance of reading' teachers' book: 'The first time the children have the books, they will be full of excitement and eager to examine the pictures'.[74] The 'Janet and John' teachers' manual included comments on the 'attractiveness' of the pictures in the series:

> The artists have avoided eccentricity or appeal to adult sophistication. The subjects are treated with direct naturalness and good taste. The colours are clear and happy, and chosen with careful regard for the appeal of the primaries to the young mind. The characters in the illustrations are usually engaged in some activity that in itself would be attractive to most children, such as sailing boats, or sliding.[75]

Some teacher's manuals explained how pictures should be used as part of the process of learning to read. Those that accompanied 'The McKee readers' in the 1950s showed the care that was taken in the organisation of the text and pictures on each page of each book in the series. The instructions presented were a kind of specification for use:

> These teacher's editions – one for each pupil's book – contain highly detailed guidance in the teaching of reading at this stage. Somewhat as an engineer's blueprints provide clear and adequate directions for the building of a great bridge, with nothing omitted from their specifications, the teacher's editions give detailed guidance for each and every piece of teaching that is essential to sound instruction in reading in the first year.[76]

The *Teacher's manual* comprised double-page spreads showing a page from the reading book and a page of related instructions for how the page should be used with the young readers. They included 'preparation', drawing attention to new words; 'reading', pointing to illustrations or title and asking questions about them; and 'word analysis', looking at the way particular words are made up of distinct sounds or letters (**58**). This level of detail and instruction indicated a close relationship between pedagogy and the content of the text and pictures. 'The royal road readers' was another 1950s scheme where the pages in the main course

73. However, research on the motivational benefits of pictures in reading books is inconclusive. Watts and Nisbet summarise research (including that undertaken by Vernon, Keir, Smith and Watkins, and Wayne and Parknas) about the motivational benefits of an illustrated as opposed to a non-illustrated text.

74. Hilda Haig-Brown and Zillah Walthew, *Romance of reading, infant series: teacher's book*, London: Oxford University Press, 1942, p. 5.

75. Munro, *A teachers' manual for use with the Janet and John reading course*, 1954, pp. 1–2.

76. P. McKee, M. Harrison, A. McCowen, and E. Lehr, *Teacher's manual for With Peter and Susan*, London: Nelson and Sons, 1955, p. x.

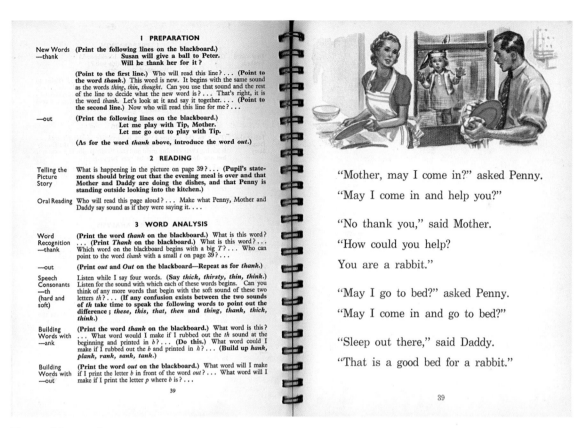

58 Spread from Paul McKee, M. Lucile Harrison, Annie McCowen and Elizabeth Lehr. 'The McKee readers', *Teacher's manual for 'With Peter and Susan'*, London: Thomas Nelson and Sons Ltd, [c.1955], spread 39. Page 203 × 149 mm.

books related closely to instructions for its use. Visually these beginner reading books had the appearance of a workbook, and must have been designed in close discussion with the authors of the scheme. On each page or spread the words or sentences were closely aligned with relevant explanatory pictures (**59**). The *Teachers' book* provided page-by-page instructions explaining the rationale, the expected behaviour of the children, and how to use wall charts, writing exercises and other supplementary apparatus.

Evelyn Goldsmith's survey of research into illustration included studies that considered the benefits of particular picture/text arrangements. Such research was inconclusive though she noted that for beginner readers it would seem that predictability of the position of an illustration in relation to the text is important. This view would also have been supported by James Kerr who in 1926 wrote that 'Only one picture to a page saves confusion. The printing of numerous small pictures in the margins is inadvisable.'[77] Some books, nevertheless, continued to be published with small pictures scattered around a double-page

77. Kerr, *The fundamentals of school health*, 1926, p.557.

59 Pages from John Clifford Daniels and Hunter Diack, 'The royal road readers', *Book one, part 1*. London: Chatto and Windus, 1959, p. 7. Page 245×186 mm.

spread such as the 'The radiant way' (1933) and 'The new star infant readers' (1940) shown in Figure **60**.

The extent to which pictures and text were integrated was of course influenced to a considerable extent by the production process.[78] In the days of metal type, wood cuts, wood-engravings and process blocks could be combined within a single printing forme, and in the nineteenth and early twentieth centuries this meant that printers could fit text and pictures around each other. When text and pictures were printed separately – such as coloured plate sections within a book – while pictures may have reflected content, they may not have been positioned next to the text to which they referred. Often the reader had to be directed to a different page. With the widespread use of offset lithography, phototypesetting and latterly desktop computers it became straightforward to integrate text and pictures.

In children's reading books typical text/picture arrangements were:

- an illustration above the text on one of the pages of a double-page spread, relating to something within the spread
- an illustration above the text on each of the pages of a spread, relating to something in the text below it
- a full-page picture on a double-page spread (usually the left-hand one), relating to something in the text opposite
- (from the mid-twentieth century onwards) integration of text and picture such that the picture/text positional relationship varied from page to page.

Aside from production constraints, such configurations might have been influenced by a particular design approach to

78. See Michael Twyman, 'The emergence of the graphic book in the nineteenth century' in R. Myers & M. Harris (eds), *A millennium of the book*, Winchester: St Paul's Bibliographies, 1994, pp. 135–80.

60 Spread from Jane Brown, 'The new star infant readers', *Book one*, Glasgow: Robert Gibson & Sons, 1940, pp. 16–17. Page 190 × 140 mm.

An example of several small pictures dotted around a spread.

the visual organisation of text and pictures (such as use of full page pictures on a right-hand or left-hand page of a spread); and consideration of how a book was intended to be used in a classroom. A typical feature of reading books for beginner readers from around the 1930s onwards was the alignment of a picture and related verbal content with a page or double-page spread.

The degree to which the pictorial narrative reflected the textual one varied. The most common relationship was where the picture provided a general context for the text. The text was thus reinforced by the picture, but equally the picture could support different (albeit similar) versions of the text. In some cases a contextual picture was inevitable because there was too much going on in the text as in Figure **61**, though an alternative solution, used relatively infrequently, was for more than one picture to be used on a page or spread, each accompanied by text that related to it, as shown in Figure **62**. Particularly in books for very early readers, the relationship between text and picture was often very direct as in the pages from a book in the 'Pilot reading scheme' in Figure **63**. Text and pictures within a double-page spread were sometimes organised to support a particular teaching method. Augusta Monteith's 1933 series, 'Child's picture readers', for example, was organised in double-page spreads with the right-hand page blank so that children could insert their own words and pictures. There was an explicit and clearly articulated rationale:

> These little books have been compiled in order to give children a supply of pictures dealing with their own everyday

61 Spread from Mabel O'Donnell and Rona Munro, 'The Janet and John books', *I went walking*, Welwyn: James Nisbet, *c*.1950, pp. 24–5. Page 198 × 138 mm.

An example of an illustration providing the general context for the text.

62 Spread from Gertrude Keir, 'Adventures in reading', *Red Indians*, London: Oxford University Press, 1946, pp. 10–11. Page 197 × 151 mm.

More than one picture on the page, each illustrating text that refers to it.

63 Spread from Pat Devenport, 'Pilot reading scheme', *The farm*, Leeds: E.J. Arnold & Sons, [1952], pp. 12–13. Page 182 × 152 mm.

A direct relationship between text and picture is typical in books for beginner readers.

64 Spread from E. S. Bradbourne, 'Through the rainbow', *Red book 3: under the table*, Huddersfield: Schofield & Sims, 1964, pp. 8–9. Page 247 × 182 mm.

In this example the right-hand page has space for the child to draw and write.

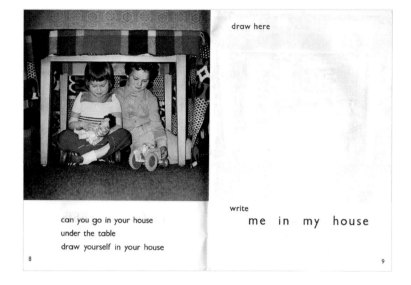

can you go in your house
under the table
draw yourself in your house

draw here

write
me in my house

experiences. It is hoped that in some schools, at any rate, they may be the personal property of the child. He could be encouraged to talk about the pictures, to give names to the children depicted in them, to write sentences of his own opposite the pictures, and to colour them in if he likes. In short, the child should build up his own special reader.[79] A similar approach was taken thirty years later in the 'Through the rainbow' series, where a photograph and related text on the verso faced a blank page with indications for drawing and copying (**64**). One problem with this approach is that every child required their own copy of the book which, in practice, was an expensive option.

79. Augusta Monteith, 'Child's picture readers', *Teacher's book*, London: London University Press, 1933, p. 20.

[1901], 181 × 122 mm

1903, 172 × 130 mm

c.1915, 180 × 123 mm

1909, 186 × 123 mm

1938, 209 × 133 mm

1946, 187 × 137 mm

65 Front covers from books published in the early part of the twentieth century showing some typical approaches.

Front and back covers

In contrast to the lively, colourful and child-friendly covers on contemporary books for teaching reading, many of those on books published before the 1950s were dreary and plain, and had a somewhat utilitarian feel. Cover designs typically included the use of a series title motif; repeat patterns; type only; and generic images associated with learning, such as the tree of knowledge, a light showing the way, steps to denote progress and children reading a book. Very few reflected the internal content; the name of the series was given prominence: the books had non-descript titles, such as *Book 1*, *First reader* and so on (**65**).

One of the changes over time is the increased visibility on the covers of the author and illustrator, as in 'The songs the letters sing' in the 1920s (**66**). Also from around this time, books within series began to have titles related to the content of the book and cover illustrations. 'Evans activity readers' in the 1940s was another series with lively and colourful covers that anticipated those from the 1960s and beyond and that prioritised the title of the book, rather than the name of the series, and named the author and illustrator (**67**). Unusually, the covers of the earliest books in the 'Pilot reading scheme' (1950s) shown in Figure **68** had no type on them.

Many publishers used the back cover to list the books in a particular series, and in some cases to present the rationale behind the series or scheme. Some examples are shown in Figure **69**; in each case the intended recipients were teachers. Some back covers were child-oriented, either through the use of pictures, or more recently, child-friendly text (**70**). A surprisingly large number of back covers were blank, or reflected the front – either exactly or in part.

66 Front cover from S. N. D. [Rose Meeres], 'The songs the letters sing', *Book II*, London and Glasgow: Grant Educational Company, [1919]. 180 × 136 mm.

This is one of the first series to give prominence to the author, S.N.D. (Sister of Notre Dame, otherwise known as Rose Meeres), and the illustrator Margaret Tarrant. The imagery of the children reading relates to the series title, with one reading child conducting the others who appear to be singing.

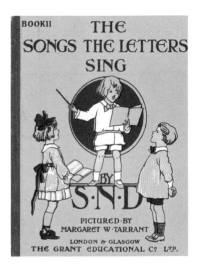

67 Front cover from 'Sunny hour stories', *The little tin train*, London: Oxford University Press, 1925. 186 × 140 mm.

Front cover from 'Evans' activity readers', *Washing*, London: Evans Brothers, [1947]. 187 × 124 mm.

Examples of covers where the titles and cover illustrations reflect the content of the books.

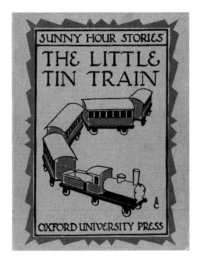

68 Front and back covers from Pat Devenport, 'Pilot reading scheme', *Pre-reader 3: The farm*, Leeds: E.J. Arnold, [1952]. Front cover 182 × 152 mm.

The rationale for producing a cover with no wording was explained in a leaflet promoting the series: 'The Pre-Reading Books with back and front covers forming a picture with no type (since the child cannot read) are intended to be "found" by the child after visits to, and talks about toyshops or farms, kitchens or post-offices.'

Book design for children's reading

69 Back covers from

'The Alexandra readers', *Two-letter primer*, London: McDougall's Educational Co, [1904]. 180 × 123 mm.

'McDougall's suggestive phonic infant readers', *First reader*, London: McDougall's Educational Co, [1900s]. 173 × 127 mm.

'Gibson's print-writing primers', The play-way book A, Glasgow: Robert Gibson & Sons, [1922]. 150 × 116 mm.

'breakthough to literacy', *Spider webs*, London: Longman Group, 1979. 184 × 124 mm.

Examples of back covers aimed primarily at teachers and that provide information about the particular series.

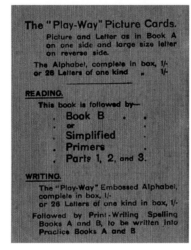
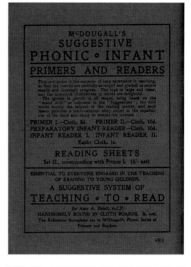
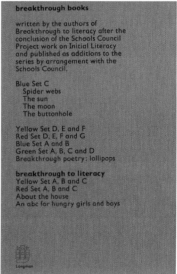

70 Back covers from

Sheila McCullagh, 'One, two, three and away!', *The cat's dance*, St Albans: Hart-Davis Educational, 1964. Illustrated by Ferelith Eccles Williams. 153 × 215 mm.

'Collins book bus', Susanna Kendall, *Will you play with me?*, London and Glasgow: Collins Educational, 1991. 160 × 135 mm.

Back covers that have been designed with the needs of children in mind.

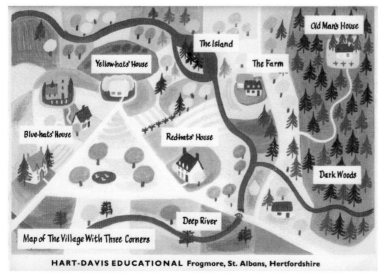

71 Spreads from three editions of
'The beacon readers'.

James H. Fassett, 'The new beacon
readers', *Book one*, London: Ginn &
Company, 1922, pp. 30–31. Illustrator
not named. Page 183 × 132 mm.

James H. Fassett, 'The beacon infant
readers'. *Book one*, London: Ginn &
Company, 1933, pp. 30–31. Illustrated by
Marcia Lane Foster. Page 183 × 132 mm.

James H. Fassett, 'The beacon readers'.
Book one, part two: At play, London:
Ginn & Company, 1955, pp. 18–19.
Illustrated by H. Radcliffe Wilson.
Page 200 × 134 mm.

Spreads from three editions with
different illustrations reflecting changing
environments and portrayal of children.

30

Ruth. Yes, the figs are in the dish.
John. Cum-je-cum.
Sam. What do you come by?
John. It begins with "c."
Ruth. Is it a cap?
John. No, it is not a cap.
Sam. Is it a cat?
John. No, it is not a cat.
Ruth. Is it a can, a tin can?
I can see a can by the pump.
John. No, it is not a can.
Sam. What can it be?
You will have to tell us.
John. It is a cup.
It stands on the shelf.

30

Ruth. Yes, the figs are in the dish.
John. Cum-je-cum.
Sam. What do you come by?
John. It begins with "c."
Ruth. Is it a cap?
John. No, it is not a cap.
Sam. Is it a cat?
John. No, it is not a cat.
Ruth. Is it a can, a tin can?
I can see a can by the pump.
John. No, it is not a can.
Sam. What can it be?
You will have to tell us.
John. It is a cup.
It stands on the shelf.

Ruth. Mother says,
"Cum-je-cum."
We say,
"What do you come by?"
Then she will tell us
how it begins.
Sam. Oh, yes. I like that.

18

Ruth. Come, Mother, begin.
Mother. Cum-je-cum.
John. What do you come by?
Mother. It begins with "d."
Ruth. Is it a doll?
Mother. No, it is not a doll.
John. Is it a dog?
Mother. No, it is not a dog.
Sam. Is it a dish?
Mother. Yes, it is a dish.

19

Different editions

Some twentieth-century reading schemes were used in schools for many decades. Sometimes these were straight reprints: to give just two examples, the last edition of the 'The Dale readers', was published in 1935, and the *Royal crown infant reader* from the 'Royal school series', popular at the beginning of the twentieth century was reprinted until at least 1945. One consequence of this was that in some schools children were learning to read from books with dated typography and illustrations. Some publishers introduced new illustrations to reflect changing fashions and attitudes to children, as can be seen, for example, across three editions of 'The Beacon readers' first published in 1922 and still being printed in 1965 (**71**). The relationship between text and pictures in the 1922 and the 1933 edition is identical; the pictures are stylistically different, and in the 1933 version the characters are portrayed more informally. Both these editions would have been printed by letterpress so the type would have been kept 'standing' and new blocks made for the pictures. In the 1955 edition, although the typography remained the same, the pages have been reformatted and additional pictures added. The group picture of the mother and the three children has been retained but additional pictures have been added to illustrate the game of cum-je-cum.

'The Radiant way' was redesigned completely in its 1967 edition (**72**). The typeface, Imprint, was replaced by a smaller size of Century Schoolbook and additional space was added between the lines. In the 1934 edition the paragraph numbering was dropped, and the keywords were distinguished from the rest of the text by being printed in red rather than underlined. One of the strongest visual changes in the later edition was a greater degree of integration of text and illustration, with pictures running across the spread. This would have been facilitated by the printing process: 4-colour offset lithography.

The main change in the 1977 edition of the 'Gay way' series, aside from the illustrative style, was in the typography (**73**), including change of typeface and reduction of word and line spacing in the later edition. The line breaks and paragraph treatment remained the same.

72 Spreads from Jane Brown 'The radiant way', *Second step*, Edinburgh: W. & R. Chambers.

1934 edition, pp. 46–7. Illustrated by Rene Cloke. Page 196 × 148 mm.

1967 edition, pp. 46–7. Illustrated by Sally Michel. Page 213 × 150 mm.

Some of the changes in these spreads from different editions are influenced by printing process: the use of colour for headings and the illustration running across both pages on a spread in the later edition. Other differences are due to dropping outdated conventions and language: numbered paragraphs and replacement of 'Wee Bob' with 'Bob'.

WORD DRILL

br

1. brag	bran	brass	brand
2. brim	bring	brick	brush

cr

3. crab	crack	crash	cross
4. crib	cress	crest	crept
5. croft	crop	crush	crust

dr

6. drank	drag	drill	drink
7. drop	dress	drum	drunk

46

<u>right</u>   <u>soldiers</u>   <u>before</u>

1. Here come the soldiers on the march. They have a brass band. Left, right! Left, right!
2. 'Come, let us play at soldiers,' said Bob to his school chums.
3. 'Jim, bring your drum. Go before us, and give us drill.
4. 'Come, lads! Left turn! Quick march! Left, right!' Crash! went the drum.
5. Wee Bob comes last of all the soldiers. He has a little drum.
6. See him cross his drum-sticks, pitter patter, pitter patter. What a happy drummer!

47

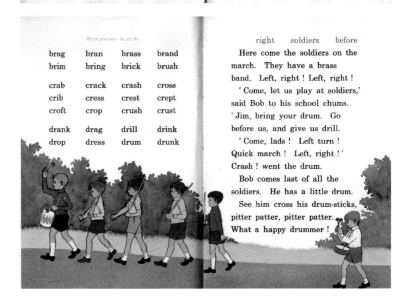

Word practice · br, cr, dr

brag	bran	brass	brand
brim	bring	brick	brush
crab	crack	crash	cross
crib	cress	crest	crept
croft	crop	crush	crust
drank	drag	drill	drink
drop	dress	drum	drunk

right   soldiers   before

Here come the soldiers on the march. They have a brass band. Left, right! Left, right!
    'Come, let us play at soldiers,' said Bob to his school chums.
    'Jim, bring your drum. Go before us, and give us drill.
    'Come, lads! Left turn! Quick march! Left, right!' Crash! went the drum.
    Bob comes last of all the soldiers. He has a little drum.
    See him cross his drum-sticks, pitter patter, pitter patter. What a happy drummer!

Occasionally different approaches to teaching reading resulted in different editions of a particular series. The 'Janet and John' books are a good example. Two sets of books were produced with almost identical pictures and stories. One set with five titles: *Off to play, Out and about, I went walking, Through the garden gate* and *I know a story*, used the 'Look and say' method; the other set, 'Janet and John', Books 1–4, had a phonic basis. In the 1960s a 'print script' edition was produced in response to teacher demand (**74**); the series was also one of those used in the i. t. a. experiment.

73 Spreads from Ella Ruth Boyce
'The gay way', *The blue book*, London:
Macmillan & Co.

1950 edition, pp. 6–7. Illustrated by
Lilian Chivers. Page 201×150 mm.

1977 edition, pp. 6–7. Illustrated by
Maureen Williams. Page 203×146 mm.

Typography and illustration style varies
in these editions. The wide word spacing
in the 1950 edition may have been a
concession to the needs of beginner
readers.

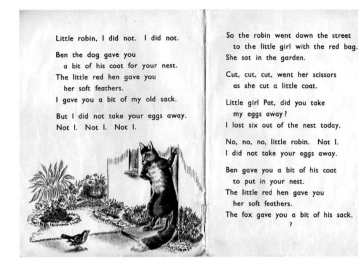

74 Spread from Mabel O'Donnell
and Rona Munro, 'The Janet and
John books', *Off to play*, Welwyn:
James Nisbet and Co, nd, *c*.1960.
Page 200×137 mm.

This 'print-script' edition is set in 24-point
Futura, with some modified characters.

A timeline of graphic attributes of reading books

The following pages show a selection of books used for teaching reading from the end of the nineteenth century to the end of the twentieth century. The timeline includes examples to show characteristic features of typography and book design in a particular period as well as innovative and distinctive approaches taken by some publishers.

The most evident change in visual organisation in books for teaching reading since the end of the nineteenth century has been the reduction of the amount of text and the number of graphic components contained within a double-page spread, such as word lists, headings and spelling exercises. A greater use of white space occurred through increased space between the lines and bigger margins. The amount of space taken up by illustrations increased. From the 1930s sanserif typefaces began to be used by some publishers, and by the 1960s most educational publishers used such letterforms for their reading schemes. Through the twentieth century there has been a shift from visual attributes determined by printing and typesetting conventions for adult readers to those more appropriate to the needs of children as beginning and emerging readers. Many publishers took account of the views of teachers and educationists, including on the use of sanserif types for continuous text; the use of infant characters; the promotion, development and use of particular typefaces; the use of wider word and line spacing than would be used in adult reading; and the use of short lines of type broken according to the meaning of the text.

Between 1890 and 1915

At the beginning of the twentieth century most reading books were set in an 18- or 24-point modern-face type; there was occasional use of old-style typefaces. Justified setting was the norm and resulted in uneven spacing between words; additional space was inserted at sentence ends. 'Chunks' of text, often just one sentence, were treated as paragraphs which were typically numbered and indented, indented with additional space, or set with the first line extended to the left as a hanging indent. Pages and spreads conformed to a 'reading lesson' that typically included a list of new words and an illustration as well as sentences for reading. Sometimes spelling exercises and handwriting specimens were included. Many books had the concluding part of one lesson on the verso, and the opening part of the next on the recto. Most books combined black-and-white and coloured illustrations, though some had coloured illustrations throughout. The most widely-used format was crown octavo (7 1/2 × 5 inches) though variation in trimming accounted for slightly different page sizes. Most books had soft covers made from cloth-covered boards; many were red printed on in black.

From 1915 to the 1930s

The impact of the 1913 *Report on the influence of school-books upon eyesight* can be seen in many books published in the latter part of the 1910s and the 1920s. Caslon and old-style typefaces in large sizes were set with tight line spacing. Some publishers chose typefaces with characteristics believed to support the reading needs of young children (such as that used in 'The songs the letters sing' which has single-storey a's and g's). The influence of the print script handwriting movement was seen through the use of handwritten forms and the occasional use of sanserif type for the main text rather than for secondary information. The 'Beacon' and 'Field' reading schemes published by Ginn introduced ideas from the USA, notably the typeface Century Schoolbook and generous use of space.

The crown-octavo format continued to be widely used though there was more variation in format to include the slightly larger demy-octavo and some smaller ones. This was a period of transition in the visual organisation of reading books: some books, for example, 'Chambers's phonic and effective' series, continued to display features redolent of those published at the end of the nineteenth century, such as numbered paragraphs and lists of new words, whereas others, such as the 'New beacon readers', anticipated future developments. The covers were typically printed in a single colour, often black, on cloth-covered board in a range of colours. The cover of *The little tin train* (1925), one of the 'Sunny hour stories', is an example of a cover with more visual interest and attractiveness.

The recommendations of the 1913 *Report on the influence of schoolbooks upon eyesight* remained evident in books published in the 1930s, such as 'Visits to storyland', but there were new approaches, as in the 'Mac and Tosh' series, where relatively small amounts of text were set in the new sanserif typefaces, Gill Sans and Granby, with ample space around the text and between the lines. Monotype faces were also in evidence, such as Imprint 101 used in 'The radiant way', as well as some unusual typefaces such as the slab serif in 'Wheaton's rhythmic readers'. By this time most reading books had coloured pictures (though not always full colour), and illustrator's names began to appear on title pages and covers of books, suggesting increased importance and status. The most common formats remained crown- and demy-octavo, and the covers typically printed in one or two colours on cloth-covered boards.

The 1940s and 1950s

In the 1940s the characteristic format for many beginner reading books in the second half of the twentieth century emerged: a picture above or alongside a small amount of generously spaced text, such as the 'The happy way to reading' and 'Activity reading scheme'. Both sanserif and serif typefaces were used, and unjustified setting resulting in even word spaces was the norm. The 1940s saw the introduction of comprehensive reading schemes, in which a series of main books was supported by supplementary readers and reading support materials such as wall charts, work books and games. A number of schemes drew on reading research. The 'Happy venture' series had a research-based rationale and was one of the first series to show reading progression through changing from sanserif to serif type.[80] The 'Royal road readers' (1954) were developed with support from the University of Nottingham. Influence from the USA was seen in the 'Janet and John' books, first published as the 'Alice and Jerry' books, and introduced after anglicisation to the UK in 1949. There began to be greater variation in format, in particular the use of small formats for supplementary books in reading schemes. Sanserif typefaces became more widely used in the 1950s, usually with ample space between the lines and around the text. Pictures began to take up more space on a double-page spread and there were some more colourful and interesting covers, such as those used for 'The McKee readers' in the 1950s.

80. See Schonell, *The psychology and teaching of reading*, 1945, pp. 20–21.

Book design for children's reading

The 1960s and 1970s

The 1960s was a period of new ideas and initiatives, many of which were teacher-initiated. The 1967 Plowden Report, with its emphasis on child-centred learning, supported such autonomy. New methods of teaching reading were supported by government funding and underpinned by university research. Research at the University of Birmingham on commonly used vocabulary in children of primary school ages resulted in the 'Queensway readers' published in the 1960s;[81] the Institute of Education, University of London played a significant role in the 1960s with testing associated with the Initial Teaching Alphabet and with 'Colour-story reading'; and University College London hosted the Schools Council research project 'Programme in Linguistics and English Teaching' directed by Michael Halliday between 1964 and 1970, which led to the 'Breakthrough to literacy' programme in the 1970s.

'Breakthrough' supported the 'whole language' approach and the view that learning to write and to read were integrated. In the early stages children were encouraged to learn to read through their own writing. A crucial difference between 'Breakthrough' and traditional reading schemes was that the teacher was in control, creating reading and writing resources through use of a 'sentence maker' that enabled children to choose and assemble words from cards to produce their own materials. In 'Breakthrough' reading books the first books that children read tended to be those that they wrote themselves. Books were organised in sets according to level and included non-fiction as well as fiction. *The teacher's manual* included lists of suitable books produced by publishers other than Longman, which also undermined the notion of a reading scheme.

The 'Breakthrough' approach was flexible and child-centred. 'Reading 360: the Ginn reading programme' (1978), which originated in the USA, also took a 'whole language' approach. The readers in the series were illustrated in different styles, and the accompanying 'magic circle' books were intentionally produced in a range of formats and had a variety of treatments of text and picture.

81. See G. E. R. Burroughs, *A study of vocabulary of young children*, London: Oliver & Boyd, 1957. The 'Queensway' scheme used words found to be in common use by children of primary school age.

1980s and beyond

The books from 'Longman reading world' (1987) continued the variation in visual appearance, using different illustrators and page designs to support a 'story method' of teaching reading. Longman was one of the few publishers to mention that 'great care has been taken throughout the scheme regarding factors that affect readability. These include … layout, spacing, and size, density and clarity of type.' [82]

With such approaches to teaching reading, and other examples including 'Collins book bus' and E. J. Arnold's 'Story chest', coloured illustrations dominated the page, often being bled off at the top and sides, even when the text was consistently positioned below. Sanserif typefaces – versions of Helvetica, Frutiger, Avant Garde Gothic, often with infant character modifications – were widely used, though some publishers, as seen in 'Cambridge reading', chose a serif typeface with infant modifications.

With the variety of formats, illustrations and text genres present in many late twentieth-century reading programmes, there was less of a visual distinction between trade children's books and educational ones, which in turn reflected the mix of books used for teaching reading in many UK primary schools.

Notes on the timeline

The books shown in the timeline are ordered more or less chronologically, though many of them were undated and continued to be published in their original form (as well as in revised editions) until well after their publication date. Along with the front cover, two double-page spreads have been selected and an actual size showing of the text in most cases. For some of the larger and more complex reading schemes produced from the middle of the twentieth century more than one book from the scheme has been selected, and has been illustrated with the cover and just one spread. Brief comments accompany each example, providing contextual information and drawing attention to salient visual characteristics.

Accurate identification of the typefaces used is not straightforward. There were, for example, many similar versions of generic modern-face types as well as named fonts such as Caslon. Gill Sans provides the clearest example of a typeface that was copied and redesigned for a number of typesetting

82. Wendy Body, 'Longman reading world', *Level 1 Teacher's book*, Harlow: Longman, 1987, p. 2.

Book design for children's reading

systems, and was endlessly customised. Letterforms that look like handwriting are likely to have been written by hand directly or produced using some form of stencil or pantograph and then transferred to a block or plate for printing.

There is a relatively stable period in the 1950s and 1960s, when the printing of books was dominated by Monotype composition, and a number of well-known designs such as Times, Perpetua, Imprint, Century Schoolbook and Gill Sans predominated. Monotype were early introducers of film typesetting, and their products maintained this stability and the design standards of metal type - so much so that it is not always easy to tell if a page was set in metal or in film, especially for designs available on both systems, such as Univers.

But as film typesetting spread in the 1970s and 1980s, new machines were introduced by companies without the typographic background of Monotype and many type designs on these machines were copies or variants of existing designs. Furthermore, now that typefaces were stored on relatively-easily copied film matrices, printers (and publishers) could produce their own versions of established typefaces, such as Univers and Helvetica, from artwork that they commissioned. Such versions typically included infant characters, such as 'I', 'a', 'g' and 'y', but the customising could also extend to other features, such as width.

Some stability returns to typeface identification with the initial introduction of digital fonts in the mid-1980s, but this was not to last. Type design and production, while still a painstaking professional task, could be undertaken on any personal computer, and existing fonts could be modified even more easily than in the days of film typesetting.

Collins school series, *The graphic infant reader. Second book,* London and Glasgow: William Collins, Sons & Company, 1891

64 pp, 176 × 120 mm

- A very popular series of primers and readers that appeared in several different editions.

- Each short section in this reader comprises up to 10 short paragraphs and is illustrated by a black-and-white wood-engraving or one of eight 'full-page coloured illustrations', a trademark feature of the series, and noted on the title page.

- Set in a 24-point modern-face type with a slab-serif form for the word list and sanserif for headings.

- Hyphens are used to denote syllables in the word list and text.

- The use of additional space between paragraphs and lines varies from page to page.

---

14 Second Infant Reader.

Ket-tle (1).

caught	killed	Ket-tle
brought	looked	bas-ket
a-sleep	mat-ter	kit-tens
go-ing	won-der	moth-er

1. The Ket-tle I am go-ing to tell you of is not the ket-tle we put on the fire. It is the odd name of our dear old cat, she is so very black—just as black as the kettle.

Second Infant Reader. 15

2. Our wee boy, Bert, gave her this name, and she has kept it. She has three kit-tens in a snug bed of hay in this bas-ket.

3. One day, when they were asleep, Kettle caught and killed a large rat.

4. She brought it to the bas-ket and gave a loud cry. All the kit-tens got up to see what was the mat-ter.

5. Then she flung the rat up, and caught it, and had a fine game, while the kit-tens looked on in won-der at their mother's tricks.

Second Infant Reader. 23

Rob at the Sea.

1. Our dog Rob went to the sea side with Rose and Tot.

2. They took off their shoes and socks, and wa-ded in the sea for some time.

3. They tried to get Rob to go in the sea too, but he did not care for it.

4. The water was too cold for his toes.

5. Soon a big boy came by and threw Rob in the sea.

6. He made a great fuss at first, but by and bye got to like it very much.

7. He can swim well now.

---

3. They tried to get Rob to go in the sea too, but he did not care for it.

4. The water was too cold for his toes.

Fowls.

chief	pick-ing	feath-ers
comb	sor-ry	fight-ing
hous-es	un-der	pil-lows
lar-ger	love-ly	health-y

1. Look at these fowls, they are of great use to us.

2. They have short, strong bills for pick-ing up grain, which is their chief food.

3. They have short wings, so they cannot fly far. They like to live under the care of man.

Page from 'Collins school series', *The graphic infant reader. Second book*, 1891

Rooster illustration with hens and roosters.

End of the 19th century

Longmans' new readers, *The infant reader: an introductory book to Standard I*, London: Longmans, Green and Co, 1886 [1891 edn]

64 pp, 180 × 123 mm

· Each lesson in this reader has the same elements: a heading; the title of the lesson in capital letters; headings 'New words' and 'Spelling lesson' in italic; a picture; and text in numbered paragraphs.

· The change in typeface from a modern typeface to a slab serif with a bold appearance to draw attention to key words has the effect of producing a disjointed page which must have been difficult to read.

· Throughout the book are pages of script for copying, reversed black to white to resemble blackboards and slates.

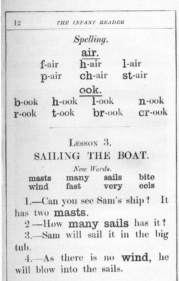

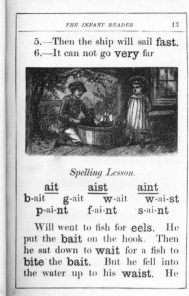

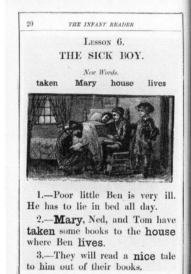

Will went to fish for **eels**. He put the **bait** on the hook. Then he sat down to **wait** for a fish to **bite** the **bait**. But he fell into the water up to his **waist**. He

Macmillan's new literary readers, *The second primer*, London: Macmillan and Co, 1895 [1902 edn]

48 pp, 170 × 116 mm

· Each short section comprises eight or nine short paragraphs preceded by a coloured or black-and-white illustration, drawn by the same illustrator.

· Set in a 24-point modern-face type with a slab-serif form for the word list.

· The vertical rules in the word list encourage vertical reading. The 'Notes to teachers' at the front of the book, however, suggest that the words 'should be read first down, then up, then across'.

· An unusual feature is the handwritten 'caption' that forms part of the illustration.

---

22   LITERARY READER

4. I had a ring on my hand, and lost it. It was the best thing I had.
5. The gun went bang, and the duck fell. It was shot in its wing.
6. The dog ran to catch the duck as it fell, and bring it to the man.
7. Fan hung her best hat on a peg. I hang my hat on the rack.
8. The bell rang for us to go to bed.
9. A duck can not sing, but a lark can.

THE SECOND PRIMER   23

Jack's duck runs in the corn. Jack will sell it, if he can.

corn	burn	hunt
horn	turn	grunt
torn	much	give
born	such	live

1. The ox is in the park. Turn it back.
2. It ran at me, and it has torn my muff with its horns.
3. I live at the big mill, by the rill.

---

32   LITERARY READER

4. Poll is a tame bird. She will take a bit of cake from my hand.
5. Bess lives in the same lane as Jane. She is lame, and can not run.
6. The cape I gave to Nell had lace on it. It came from the best shop.
7. Ben has ten pens. Tell him to save six for me.
8. We must not sit on the sand. It is wet with the waves.
9. Dan and Ben had a game in the cave.

THE SECOND PRIMER   33

Let us run to the mill as fast as we can go.

Kate	hate	bare	fare
gate	mate	care	hare
late	slate	dare	mare

1. Kate sat on a gate. She fell off, and it made her lame.
2. Sam made a mark on his slate with a pen.

---

4. Poll is a tame bird. She will take a bit of cake from my hand.
5. Bess lives in the same lane as Jane. She is lame, and can not run.

End of the 19th century

Nellie Dale, **The Dale readers**, *Steps to reading*, London: George Philip & Son, *c.*1900
Illustrations: Walter Crane

First published in 1899 as 'The Walter Crane readers', a series of seven primers and readers that promote the 'Dale method of teaching reading' which uses colour to represent particular sounds. The method is described in detail in Nellie Dale,

On the teaching of English reading, London: George Philip, 1899. The series was illustrated with large and small illustrations in full colour by Walter Crane. It was reprinted in many editions.

Nellie Dale, **The Dale readers**, *Steps to reading, c.*1900
16 pp, 181 × 122 mm

· The use of a sanserif typeface as the primary font in *Steps to reading* was innovative, specified by Dale because she thought it was similar to handwritten letterforms. The spreads illustrated here show the different grots used in two editions.

Nellie Dale, **The Dale readers**,
*Second primer, c.*1900

44 pp, 181 × 122 mm

· Most of the books in the series are
set in 24-point Antique Old Style,
with word lists set in a grot.

· The main text is set justified with
indented paragraphs and is run
around small illustrations.

34.

rich   tinge   hinge
which   singe   fringe

Dan will trot on his
nag to Kingston and get
a man to singe it.

Dan will then visit the
doll shop and get Lily
that wax doll which is
in a pink dress.

When Dobbin trotted
back the
hills had a
red tinge,
as the sun
was setting.

35.

limp crimp shrimp

Tim has a bad leg and
limps along.

Jack will pat him and
tell him to rest in his
kennel till his leg gets
well. Tim will lick
Jack's hand.

Dick and Jack will
get shrimping nets
and run to
the sands.
Jack wants
to get his
bucket full
of shrimps.

pack   tax
packing   taxing

bang   bank
banging   banking

flash   camp
flashing   camping

wash   want
washing   wanting

28.

Neddy was stamping.
Dobbin was splashing.
The duck was quacking.
The cat was washing.

29.

bill   mill   hill
kill   rill   chill
gill   fill   gill

That rill runs to the
mill which is on the
hill. Lily fell into the
rill and got a chill.

Fanny will fill a cup
with hot milk and send
it up to Lily.

Jack's cat is sitting
on the bed.
Nan will
fetch it a
gill of milk.

Jack will pat him and tell him to rest in his kennel till his leg gets well. Tim will lick Jack's hand.

The Alexandra readers,
Two-letter primer, London
and Edinburgh: McDougall's
Educational Co, 1901

16 pp, 180 × 123 mm

· A short booklet for beginner
readers that would have been
read alongside the related
'Two-letter reading sheets'. The
series is described on the back
cover: 'The LESSONS are varied
and comprehensive, embracing
everything that can interest and
instruct; the ILLUSTRATIONS in
colour and black-and-white are a
special feature and quite unrivalled
in their excellence; ... the CLEAR
PRINTING and STRONG BINDING
increase the value of the series.'

· The typography is unusual: a
24-point slab serif (unbracketed)
set centred with even, wide spaces
between the words.

· The text on each page is preceded
by an illustration that does not
relate to the content.

· The content is somewhat
constrained by use of only 2-letter
words and many of the sentences
do not make sense.

· Two spot colours, orange and
yellow, are used mainly for
background in the illustrations.

8 TWO-LETTER PRIMER.

Me. me. We. we.
Is it on an ox?
No, it is on me.
Is an ox at me? No.
We go to an ox.
If it is in we go in.
We go at it so.
No, no, it is at me.

TWO-LETTER PRIMER. 9

He. he. Be. be.
Is he on? No, I am on.
He is in it as I am.
Am I to be on it?
No, Jo is to be on.
Be at it as I am.
We go in if it be in.
He is at it if we go.

4 TWO-LETTER PRIMER.

At. at. As. as.
I am at an ox.
Am I on an ox? No.
Am I at an ox?
No, I go on an ox.
Am I as an ox?
No, on an ox am I.
Jo, go as I go.

TWO-LETTER PRIMER. 5

Is. is. It. it.
Is an ox on?
No, Jo is on an ox.
I am on, so is an ox.
It is an ox. So it is.
Go on ox as I am on.
Is it as it is?
Jo is at it so.

Is it on an ox?
No, it is on me.
Is an ox at me? No.
We go to an ox.

The press-forward readers,
Second primer, London:
O. Newmann & Co, *c.*1900s
72 pp, 186 × 123 mm

· An example of a reading book produced by a non-mainstream educational publisher, which may account for some unusual features: the illustration separates the word list from the main narrative in the first lessons in the book; in the first part of the book capital letters are used only for headings and initial capitals in proper nouns.

· Set in a bold modern-face type with very tight line spacing.

· No attempt is made to align the components of the reading lesson with pages or spreads.

· Black printing is used throughout.

8   SECOND PRIMER.

LESSON 6.
ack

sack	Jack
back	slack
pack	black

1. Jack will fill the sack with sand.
2. then Tom will put it on his back.
3. Tom will run up the hill with the sack.
4. the man at the mill has a big sack.
5. the black hen will get at the stack.
6. this man has a pack on his back.
7. it is a big pack, and the man can not run with it.

SECOND PRIMER.   9

LESSON 7.

ick	rick	stick
pick	wick	chick
lick	brick	thick

1. the dog is fond of Dick, and will lick his hand.
2. it will run and pick up a stick.
3. it can not pick up a brick.
4. it can swim in the pond.
5. it went with Dick in the gig, and sat on his lap.
6. it is not a big dog, but it can pick up a thick stick.
7. the hen and the chick can pick at the rick.
8. Dick and his dog sat on the rick.

64   SECOND PRIMER.

4. Jack cannot sow the seeds, for the wind blows them away.
5. The trees and the grass bend low.
6. The birds do not sing, but have flown to hide in the trees.
7. I fear the nests in the trees will be blown to bits.
8. The brook flows fast, and the man cannot fish in it.
9. The hens cannot scratch, so we will take them a bowl of food.
10. Then we will sit by the fire and read.
11. The wind makes the fire glow.

SECOND PRIMER.   65

all

ball	wall	
fall	hall	stall
aw	saw	
caw	claw	
paw	draw	straw

A WET DAY.

1. When it is wet we play in the hall.
2. We can play at ball, and at hide and seek.
3. We can run from wall to wall.

1. the dog is fond of Dick, and will lick his hand.
2. it will run and pick up a stick.
3. it can not pick up a brick.
4. it can swim in the pond.
5. it went with Dick in the gig, and sat on his lap.

Chambers's twentieth century readers, *First primer arranged on the word-building principle*, London and Edinburgh: W. & R. Chambers, *c*.1905

32 pp, 180 × 122 mm

· One of a series comprising two primers, two infant readers and Books I to IV relating to each of the Standards. It is a typical example of an early twentieth-century book for beginner readers with a picture and word list preceding numbered sentences on each page. The series is described on the back cover: 'All the books are written in a bright and attractive style, and have been Specially Illustrated in Colour and in Black-and-White by some of the most prominent artists of the day.'

· The main text is set in a 24-point modern-face type. A bold version is used for the word lists.

· Like many of the first books in series produced at this time, the preliminary pages showed the alphabet in different forms. The spread shown here groups small letters and capitals according to shape.

at	f-at	p-at
b-at	h-at	r-at
c-at	m-at	s-at

1. The fat cat sat on the mat.
2. Can we pat it? We can.
3. The cat ran at the rat.
4. The rat ran in-to the hat.
5. It is my hat, and my cat.
6. Fan can go to the fat cat, and pat it. So can Nan.
7. My bat is on the mat, by the cat.

-ad	l-ad	s-ad	l-ap	r-ap
b-ad	m-ad	-ap	m-ap	s-ap
h-ad	p-ad	c-ap	n-ap	t-ap

1. Dan is in the van. He is a bad lad, so I am sad.
2. Dan is a bad lad, to rap Fan.
3. Fan and I sat in the van, and had a nap.
4. Dan ran to rap Fan, as she sat in the van.
5. I had a cap and a pad on my lap; Fan had a map.

ALPHABET—SMALL LETTERS.
(Grouped according to Shape.)

1. o c e
2. s a
3. i r u n m
4. v w x z
5. l d b h k
6. t f
7. j p q y g

ALPHABET—CAPITAL LETTERS.
(Grouped according to Shape.)

1. O C G Q
2. I L T F E
3. V W A N M
4. H K X Y Z
5. U S J
6. P B R D

1. Dan is in the van. He is a bad lad, so I am sad.
2. Dan is a bad lad, to rap Fan.
3. Fan and I sat in the van, and had a nap.

b-ark   l-ark   h-ave
d-ark   m-ark   g-ive
h-ark   p-ark   l-ive

1. The sun is up. Let us have a run in the park.
2. Hark to the song of the lark! Can it not sing well?
3. Has the lark a nest?

Page from 'Chambers's twentieth century readers', *Second primer arranged on the word-building principle, c.*1905

The Palmerston series, *The sight and sound primer II*, London and Glasgow: Blackie & Son, *c*.1905

48 pp, 174 × 118 mm

· Each short section comprises eight or nine short paragraphs preceded by a coloured or black-and-white illustration, drawn by the same illustrator.

· Set in an 18-point modern-face type with a bold variant used for the top row in the word lists.

· The text is divided into numbered sections, in this case each is a sentence. The use of parentheses around the number and reduction in type size is an unusual feature.

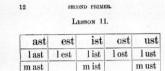

12　　SECOND PRIMER.

LESSON 11.

ast	est	ist	ost	ust
l ast	l est	l ist	l ost	l ust
m ast		m ist		m ust
f ast		f ist		

(1) The ship is lost in the mist.
(2) I was the last to see the mast.

(3) The ship must not go fast, lest it get on to a rock.

SECOND PRIMER.　　13

LESSON 12.

ast	est	ist	ost	ust
c ast			c ost	
	r est			r ust
	b est			b ust

Look and say— off.

(1) There is rust on this lock.
(2) Dick must do the best he can to get it off; then he can rest.

(3) I cast the net in,to the dock and it was lost. (4) Can you tell me the cost of the net?

42　　SECOND PRIMER.

LESSON 41.

WORD-BUILDING.

1. ill	2. ack	3. ick	4. uck	5. and
t ill	t ack	t ick	t uck	t and
st ill	st ack	st ick	st uck	st and
	st ack s	st ick s		st and,ing
6. ank	7. ink	8. unk	9. ing	10. ung
t ank	t ink	t unk	t ing	t ung
st ank	st ink	st unk	st ing	st ung
	st ink,ing		st ing s	
11. amp	12. ump	13. int	14. art	15. ern
t amp	t ump	t int	t art	t ern
st amp	st ump	st int	st art	st ern
st amp s	st ump s	st int s	st art s	
16. orm	17. ill	18. ank	19. ink	20. unk
t orm	r ill	r ank	r ink	r unk
st orm	shr ill	shr ank	shr ink	shr unk
st orm s			shr ink s	
21. ill	22. ull	23. irt	24. ist	25. ar
k ill	k ull	k irt	w ist	c ar
sk ill	sk ull	sk irt	tw ist	sc ar
	sk ull s	sk irt s	tw ist,ing	sc ar f

SECOND PRIMER.　　43

LESSON 42.

(1) "Stick on this stamp, Dick, and run to post.
(2) "If you are quick you will just catch it.
(3) "Do not stand there; the storm will not hurt you"
(4) But Dick did not start.
(5) In his hand he held a whip. He did so wish to put a lash to it.
(6) "Run along, Dick." Still Dick did not go.
(7) Then the stick fell on his back with a smart cut.
(8) Ah, Dick! you had to start then.

(1) There is rust on this lock.
(2) Dick must do the best he can to get it off; then he can rest.

Blanche Hanbury Rowe,
Rowe's rapid method of teaching reading, *The second primer*, London: J. M. Dent & Co, 1909

Illustrations: P. B. Hickling, D. Curtiss and the author

48 pp, 186 × 123 mm

- A primer set in a 14-point modern-face type, which is smaller than contemporary 'second primers', resulting in very text-heavy pages.

- Long word lists set in a sanserif typeface precede the text in each section; letters that do not sound are crossed through.

- Sanserif type is also used for tables of word lists at the end of the book, showing how consonants combine with other letters.

- Coloured illustrations are used throughout, though not on each spread.

---

4   SECOND PRIMER.

PICKING DAISIES.

die	tie	dry	try	cry
died	tried	dried*	tried	cried
lady	baby	daisy	we tidy	tidi-ly
ladies*	babies	daisies	she tidies	

1. [May and Lucy go out with Fanny to pick daisies.]

Fanny did pick a lot. But she let them lie in the sun, till the sun dried them up. And so the daisies died.

When Fanny saw that the daisies had

* *When y changes to ie, the i has the same sound (of long i, or short i) which the y had.*

PART I.   5

died, she cried. And she said, crossly, "You nasty daisies"; and she threw them in the mud.

It is sad to see such a thing as that.

Lucy and May picked daisies too, and tried to string them into a daisy-chain to go on baby's neck.

And May, as she picked the daisies, laid them in wet moss, so as not to let them die.

But when she saw how Fanny cried, May tied up a few of them in moss, and laid them in Fanny's lap.

Then Fanny said, "Oh, thank you, May."

And now she will not be so silly as to cry and be cross.

play	stay	stop	kiss	miss
played	stayed	stopped	kissed	missed
fill	will	pick	peck	pack
filled	willed	picked	pecked	packed
beg	rig	trim	cross	fish
begged	rigged	trimmed	crossed	fished

---

14   SECOND PRIMER.

THE BROOD OF CHICKS.

coop	room	boot	pool	moon	roof	food
scoop	broom	root	tool	noon	hoof	rood
loop	groom	hoot	stool	spoon	woof	brood
poop	boom	shoot	fool	boon	swoon	mood
stoop	loom	coot	cool	coon	tooth	bloom
swoop	doom	loot	school	bal-loon	sooth	gloom

6. May came into the kitchen to get food for the new brood. "You must boil an egg," said Mammy, "scoop out the inside, and chop it quite fine. Egg is best to feed chickies with, and a root of chick-weed as green food."

"How can a chicken eat," said Davy, "if it has no tooth?"

"You will soon see," said May, "if you stoop down when you get to the hen coop."

"Tell Amy, if she wishes to see them, she must go in thick boots," said Mammy, "because it has been raining."

"Amy is in a gloomy mood," said Lucy,

PART I.   15

"she sits on a stool in the schoolroom, and says it is too hot to go out at noon-day."

"How foolish!" said May. "Next she will say it is too cool to go out in the moonshine. I will show Amy three wee chickies that cannot peck yet, and must be fed with a spoon. Then she will soon wish to see the rest of the brood."

And Amy went; and just in time to res-cue a tiny chick from drowning in a rain-pool.

"How foolish!" said May. "Next she will say it is too cool to go out in the moonshine. I will show Amy three wee chickies that cannot peck yet, and must be fed with a spoon. Then she will soon

Between 1900 and 1915

Laura L. Plaisted (ed.),
The Oxford reading books,
Infant reader I, London: Oxford
University Press, *c*.1915

80 pp, 180 × 123 mm

· Set in an 18-point modern-face
type.

· The text is set justified with
indented paragraphs. Much of the
narrative is reported speech so
there is rather more punctuation
than is typically the case in books of
this kind.

· Black-and-white and colour
illustrations are interspersed
throughout though not on every
page.

28   FIRST INFANT READER

LESSON 12.—*ar*.

MR. MARSH, THE FARMER.

"Mr. Marsh has asked us to go
and see his garden," said Mother.
"We had better go on. the car ; it
is too far for Alfred's legs ! We
will start at ten o'clock, and we
can go to the market on the way
home."

Mr. Marsh was a farmer. He had
a charming garden, as well as a
farm. Mother and the children
were glad to go with him into the
farmyard, and then to the garden.

"Come and see my orchard," he
said. "You can pick up the
apples and plums if you like, Alfy."

Then he gave Alfred and Hilda
a ride in his cart, and at last
Mother said they must go home.

A RIDE IN THE FARMER'S CART

14   FIRST INFANT READER

"See, Hilda ! Kitty is running
after her tail !"

But Hilda laid her dolly by the
side of the train, and ran into the
kitchen to see Mother.

When Father came home to
dinner the rain had quite stopped,
so the children went with him to
the gate.

LESSON 6.—*ay*.

EDDY AND MAY.

"Can Eddy come to-day, Mother?"
asked Alfred.

"Yes," said Mother. "It is fine
to-day. Ask him to bring May ;
she will like to play with Hilda."

Eddy is Alfred's play-mate, and
May is his little sister.

So Alfred fetched Eddy and

FIRST INFANT READER   15

May, and the four children had
a gay time.

Alfred's Father gave them a ride
on Dapple, the gray mare. Then
they had a game with Tray, the
big black and white dog. He lay

Mr. Marsh was a farmer. He had
a charming garden, as well as a
farm. Mother and the children
were glad to go with him into the
farmyard, and then to the garden.

Eleanor I. Chambers, **Blackie's new systematic English readers**, *First infant reader*, London and Glasgow: Blackie and Son, [1913–24]

96 pp, 205 × 135 mm

· A series comprising two phonic primers, two phonic infant readers and six readers relating to the Standards.

· Set in 24-point Antique Old Style.

· From the inside front cover: 'An entirely new departure has been made in format, a large page with large type well spaced having been adopted in full conformity with the recommendations of the British Association Committee specially appointed to enquire into the print of schoolbooks in relation to children's eyesight.'

· As with many books with colour plate sections, the illustrations do not always relate to the facing text pages, as shown here where the reader is directed to page 24 for the story about the pet lamb.

---

64   FIRST INFANT READER

4. "Be quick, Peter," said Mr. Palmer, "or you will be late for your class, and Kate will be late too."

5. But, Peter was watching the motes dancing in the sun; so he was late, and could not sit by his mate, Jack.

6. He had to bring a note back, to ask his dad to send him at two o'clock.

___

PETER AND KATE
Part II

1. Kate was not late; she had her slate, and she got to the gate long before Peter did.

PETER AND KATE   65

2. She had to write a note, to ask for some white shoes to drill in.

3. Peter can write too, but not so well as Kate. He has a flute, and can skate on the pond.

4. The skates were in an old crate at the tin-shop;

THE PET LAMB
(Page 24)

IN THE PUNT   27

IN THE PUNT

1. Alfred Dench is Dick's chum; and he has come from York, all by himself, to see Jack and Dick.

2. They will let him go in the punt with them, to Teddington; but they must all sit still, or the punt will tilt.

3. They saw a calf on the bank, and some men, in punts, fishing for tench; but they did not see them catch any.

4. At last, they got to Teddington Lock; and they went in. Then the lock-man shut up the lock; and they had to

---

1. Once, a farmer and two men went to a cattle market to sell a bull; but the bull ran

S. N. D. [Rose Meeres],
The songs the letters sing,
Book I, London and Glasgow:
Grant Educational Co, *c*.1919/20
Illustrated by Margaret Tarrant
64 pp, 180 × 136 mm

· A very popular series that was used in schools at least until the 1940s. It comprised three main books and two 'bridge readers' illustrated opposite.

· The main books are set in a bold almost monolinear roman similar to Cheltenham Bold, described in notes to the teacher on the back cover as being 'especially recommended as causing as little eye strain as possible.'

· There is considerable variation in word and line spacing, and also type size, to get the text to fit around the illustrations and within a page.

· Red is used on some of the pages to draw attention to new letter combinations.

· The books are profusely illustrated by Margaret Tarrant. The use of numerous small illustrations on some of the pages, and the variation in the alignment and spacing of the type as a result, produces some visually confusing pages.

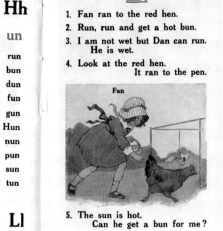

S. N. D. [Rose Meeres],
The songs the letters sing,
Book IIA, London and Glasgow:
Grant Educational Co, *c.*1919/20
Illustrated by Margaret Tarrant
64 pp, 180 × 136 mm

· The 'bridge' readers between books I and II were set in an unusual 24-point typeface, probably an Edwardian jobbing one. It bears some resemblance to Richmond Old Style which appeared in a 1925 specimen issued by the Blackfriars type foundry.

· The infant characters seem to have been specially drawn to supplement the other characters.

· This typeface is described in the introduction as being 'a bold script ... helpful for writing as well as reading'.

Chambers's phonic and effective series, *Chambers's first primer*, London and Edinburgh: W. & R. Chambers, Ltd, 1920

32 pp, 198 × 140 mm

· The book's Preface contains reference to the BAAS 1913 guidelines: 'An important feature of this set of phonic primers and infant readers is the employment of large and well-spaced type ... this has necessitated the use of a comparatively large page size, but one not, it is hoped, beyond the capacity of little hands to hold'.

· Set in 24-point Antique Old Style with generous word and line spacing.

· There is no typographic differentiation between word lists and the sentences that follow.

an	man	tan	Dan	to
can	pan	van	Fan	the
fan	ran	and	Nan	

1. The man in a van is Dan.
2. Nan ran up to the van.
3. Nan can fan Dan.
4. The fan is on the can.
5. The can is in the pan.
6. Fan ran to Dan and Nan.
7. Fan is at the van; Nan is in the van.

| at | cat | hat | pat | sat |
| bat | fat | mat | rat | Pat |

1. A fat cat sat in a van.
2. The fat cat sat on a mat.
3. A rat ran in-to the van.
4. The fat cat ran at the rat.
5. The rat ran in-to a can.
6. The cat is at the can.
7. Nan can pat the fat cat.
8. Pat sat on a bat in the van. Fan sat on a mat.

-op	pop	ox
hop	sop	box
mop	top	fox

1. Dot is my dog. He has a big dot on his leg.
2. I can hop; Dot can not.
3. Dot has his bed in a box. If the top is not on the box, in he can pop.
4. The top of the box is wet. Get a mop to it, Fan.

Revisal Lesson.

1. Has Tom got a pet?
2. Yes, he has a dog, a cat, a big red fox, and a pet hen. Has he not a lot?
3. As the red fox is in a big pen, it can-not rob Tom of his pet hen.
4. The hen is in its pen.
5. The pen has a box in it. The hen can hop on to the top of the box.

1. The man in a van is Dan.
2. Nan ran up to the van.
3. Nan can fan Dan.
4. The fan is on the can.

Nelson's phonic primer, London: Thomas Nelson & Sons Ltd, [1920s]

48 pp, 186 × 138 mm

Illustrations: Bessie Darling Inglis

· Set in a 24-point Old Style that resembles Miller & Richard Old Style but with a very large x-height.

· Each short 'lesson' comprises numbered paragraphs of one or two sentences.

· New words are enclosed in blue and red boxes and set in a bold version of the text typeface. Blue boxes denote phonic breakdown of words, the red boxes show new whole words.

· A coloured illustration in a range of sizes accompanies each lesson.

[26]

4. Shall we shut the shed? Yes, the black cat must not get in.
5. The black cat is as fond of fish as Bess is.

LESSON 24.

| fl ag | fl at | fl ash | fl ing |
| fl ap | fl ed | fl ock | fl ung |

1. Bill has a ship with a mast and a flag. It is at the end of the pond. See the flag flap in the wind!
2. The ship is sharp at the end. It can go fast. We shall see it cross the pond.

[27]

3. Jim flung a bit of brick at it. He must not do that. It will sink the ship.
4. I see a flat chip on the sand. That will be my ship. Get a short mast to set up on it.
5. Tom had a shell for his ship, but it sank in the pond.

[18]

LESSON 16.

· ash	· ish	· ush
l ash	d ish	g ush
r ash	fish	h ush
s ash	w ish	r ush

1. Bess has a red sash. I wish to get a sash for Nan.
2. Nan is fond of pink; she has a pink hat.
3. Hush! do not tell her yet that she is to get a sash.
4. That lad has fish to sell. He is a rash lad. Tell him not to lash his ass.
5. The ass can-not rush up a hill with a cart of fish.

[19]

LESSON 17.

| bl ack | bl ush |
| bl ock | bl unt |

| this | your |

1. This is Nan with her pink sash and her black hat.
2. Sit on that block of fir, Nan. Do not blush, and do not tug at your sash.
3. Nan has a long pin in her hat. The pin is to fix on her big hat.
4. Is it a blunt pin? No, it is not. Bess has just hurt her hand with it.

Sit on that block of fir, Nan. Do not blush, and do not tug at your sash.

Gibsons print-writing primers, *The play-way book B*, Glasgow: Robert Gibson & Sons, *c*.1922

32 pp, 150 × 116 mm

· A series comprising alphabet books and primers that use a phonic approach. The reading scheme is linked to Gibson's print-script handwriting scheme, which is referred to in the title.

· Set in a 24-point grot with infant characters. Another edition using the same text and pictures, *The beginner's book, B,* is produced with 'ordinary-print type letters for a, g and t instead of the print-writing characters a, g and t'.

· Two-colour illustrations in a range of formats are used throughout.

ag	ag : ip : om	T t
ip	bag : lip : Tom	Ted
om	rag : dip : and	Tip
	wag : sip : pom	

a pig and a pom.

1. Tip is a pom.
2. a pom is a dog.
3. it is not a big dog.
4. not as big as a pig.
5. the man had a pig in his bag.
6. but Tom cut the bag, and let the pig sup in the bin.

at	h..at	hat	P p
	s..at	sat	Pat
	p..at	pat	
	m..at	mat	

on a mat : in a hat.

is it a cat ?
it is a cat.
it is a fat cat.
a fat cat on a mat.

a cat sat in a hat.
in a hat! is it in it ?
it is, pat it.

a cat sat on a mat, in a hat.

5. the man had a pig in his bag.

6. but Tom cut the bag, and let the pig sup in the bin.

Gibson's simplified print writing primer, *Stage 3*, Glasgow: Robert Gibson and Sons, *c.*1922

96 pp, 190 × 136 mm

- The back cover of this primer has a note: 'This book conforms in arrangement and size of Type with the recommendations made by the British Association for the Advancement of Science.' While the size and the spacing align, the use of a sanserif typeface is not part of those recommendations, and it is that feature that is particularly distinctive about this series.

- Set in a 24-point grot with infant characters 'a', 'g' and 't'. The reference to 'print-writing' in the title suggests that this typeface was chosen to replicate as closely as possible the print script handwriting that was being taught in some schools.

- Black and white illustrations occur throughout, though not on every spread.

---

18   The lost six-pen·ce.

6. "Gee up, hors-es!" and Tom crack·ed his whip to make them go fast-er.

7. But a pur·se is not like a whip; it can o-pen.

8. Just then, the spring lost its catch, and the six-pen·ce shot o-ver the top of the brid·ge in-to the riv-er.

9. Alas! it was quite lost.

10. Moth-er was sad to think her lad was so care-less.

11. Tom made up his mind to do bet-ter next time.

12. Sin·ce then, he has lost no more six-pen·ces.

The blind girl.   19

Vowel long before **nd, ld,** and **gh** silent.

Drill.

find	old	high	light
blind	bold	sigh	sight
wild	sold	might	light
child	told	night	fright

Practice.

Ma-ry	school	smile·d
there	step·ped	less-ons
where	for-ward	gen-tle-man

: Story 6. :: The blind girl. :

Look and say—**eyes.**

1. Is it not sad to be blind!

2. This lit-tle girl can-not see the sun-light or the sky.

3. But still she is bright and cheery. Her name is Ma-ry. Has she not a nice face?

---

26   Phonic Primer—3.

4. Three girls were seen run-ning hith-er and thith-er, call-ing the child's name.

5. Dot had tod-dle·d off by her-self, and had man-age·d to scram-ble on to a wall, at the bot-tom of which ran a deep ditch.

6. "Oh! yon-der she is."

Dot on the wall.   27

7. "Do not call her name; if you do, she will fall!"

8. Farm-er Smith then went for-ward on tip-toe, and got hold of Dot be-fore she had time to see him.

9. "There, lit-tle one, this is no place for you." And he hand-ed Dot to her sis-ters.

Drill.   **a** as **a**W after **W.**

war	ward	wand	wa-ter
warn	was	want	wan-der
warm	wasp	watch	wal-nut
swarm	wash	what	war-ble

Practice.

lis-tens	to-geth-er	as-sist
sec-ond	class-es	march-es
com-mands	class-work	ad-vance

---

her-self, and had man-age·d to scram-ble on to a wall, at the bot-tom of which ran a deep ditch.

James. H. Fassett, **The new beacon readers**, *Book one*, London: Ginn and Company, 1922

60 pp, 183 × 132 mm

· The 'New beacon readers' originated in the United States and were produced in Britain between 1922 and 1928. In the 1930s they were re-published as 'The beacon infant readers' and they remained in print, in several editions, for many years.

· Set in 24-point Century Schoolbook, ranged-left setting with one sentence per line.

· There is no typographic differentiation of new words that precede some of the reading passages.

· Distinctive coloured illustrations are used throughout.

baby   says

Mother, see baby.
See baby play ball.
Baby can catch the ball.
See baby catch it.
It is my ball.
Can you see us, mother?
Baby can play ball.
Baby says, "Baby can play ball."

Kitty is in my lap.
See baby pat the kitty.
Baby says, "Kitty, little kitty."
It is a fat little kitty.
Baby likes to pat the kitty.
Mother, do see baby and kitty.

picnic   car   day

John.   O mother, I am so hot!
Sam.   Rover is hot, too.
John.   May we have a picnic?
     Do let us, mother.
Mother.   Yes, John, if you like.
     You may have a picnic.
John.   Baby will like it.
     It is a good day for a picnic.
Sam.   May I come, too?
     May I come to the picnic?
Mother.   Yes, you may come, Sam.
     Ruth, will you come, too?
     Father will take us in a car.

NOTE. *Picnic* may be taught in syllables phonetically.

Kitty is in my lap.
See baby pat the kitty.
Baby says, "Kitty, little kitty."
It is a fat little kitty.

school   begun   write

Ring, ting, ting!
The little bell will ring.
School has begun,
And it is fun
To read and write and sing.

NOTE. Study the tables on p. 59 to prepare for later reading.

Page from 'The new beacon readers', *Book one*
1922

New steps for tiny folk,
E. A. Gregory, *Two little runaways*, London: Oxford University Press, 1926

12 pp, 185 × 145 mm

Illustrations: Winifred Ackroyd

· One of a series of twelve books intended to follow the related series' 'First steps for tiny folk' and 'Easy steps for tiny folk'.

· Each series is set justified in 24-point Caslon which results in very variable word spacing that is increased at sentence ends.

· Black printing throughout and a self-cover makes this a low-cost series. 'Easy steps' shown below uses a second colour on the cover and in the illustrations.

As they went they met a dog. He was called Tray.

"Tray, Tray, we are running away to play and dig on the sands. You may come with us and bring a pail too. Will you come with us, Tray?"

"No," said Tray. "I cannot come. I have no pail, and I cannot come with you to play and dig on the sands. I cannot get away from my chain. I must stay in my kennel."

So Sam and Pip ran on.

Next they met a little red hen.

"We are running away to play and dig on the sands," said Sam and Pip. "You may come with us, little red hen, and bring a little pail. Will you come with us?"

"No," said the little red hen. "I live with the cat

Ducky Lucky," they said. "Will you bring a pail and come to play and dig on the sands with us?"

"No," said Ducky Lucky. "I cannot come to play and dig on the sands with you to-day. I cannot run as fast as you can. I shall stay and swim in this pond with my little ducklings."

So off ran Sam and Pip to play and dig on the sands.

III

On the way they met a robin.

"Hullo, little robin," said Sam and Pip. "We are running away to play with this pail and dig on the sands to-day. Will you come with us, little robin?"

"No," said Baby Robin. "I must stay in the nest and wait till my mother comes

cannot come. I have no pail, and I cannot come with you to play and dig on

"Good dog, Bob," says Jim. "Now you can beg for a bit of bun."

So Bob begs for it. Jim lets him get a big bit. Jim has a duck too. The duck is Tom. Jim is fond of Tom, but not so fond as he is of Bob.

Tom can-not run as fast as Bob. He can-not beg, but he can swim in the pond, and he can dig in the mud with his bill. He can say "Quack, quack," too.

If Jim runs to the pond, Tom will say, "Quack, quack."

Jim will let him get a bit of bun if he says, "Quack, quack."

Jim has a hen too. It is a big hen.

The hen is Bess. Bess can-not beg, but she can lay an egg for Jim.

Jim will let Mum fry the egg for Dad's tea.

Jim has a rabbit too. The rabbit is Sam. Sam is in the big hut in the yard. Sam is a big rabbit. He has fur on him. He has a wee tail. If Sam runs, his tail bobs up. So Jim calls him "Bob-tail."

Bob-tail can run fast. He can run faster than Jim. He can run faster than Bob the dog. Bob will run at him, but he can-not get him.

Jim has a big cat and a

wee kitten. The big cat is Tib. Tib is the mother of the kitten.

The kitten is Rags. Jim says Rags is the best pet of all.

Rags can run up a tree, and so can the mother cat. Rags can jump. So can Tib.

Sunny hour stories, *The little tin train*, London: Oxford University Press, 1925

32 pp, 186 × 140 mm

· One of a series of six books.

· Set in 18-point Caslon Bold.

· Short lines and even word spacing combined with generous space between the lines results in a page that is not intimidating to read. The approach taken to the typography is similar to that taken in the 'Beacon readers' so the series may have had origins in the USA.

· Each spread contains one or two two-colour illustrations.

"Do not go away,"
said Little Boy Blue.
"Stay and live with me."

"I had a good play,
I had a good play;
but I can not stay,"
said the Little Tin Train.

Then with a "Too, too, too!"
and a "Choo, choo, choo!"
away went the Little Tin Train.

It ran back to the toy shop,
and jumped into the box
where it lived.

10

Singing to the King

A Hen, a Duck, and a Goose
lived in the King's barn yard.
They had more food
than they could eat.
But they would not give
Wee Robin a seed.

11

Winkie was fast caught
in a hole in the fence.

30

Peter and Pinkie
tried to help her.

Peter pulled her legs,
and Pinkie pulled her tail.
They pulled and pulled.
They pulled
till Winkie was free.
Then Winkie lay down
on the grass to rest.

Winkie had no tail.
Pinkie had pulled it off.
Peter said,
"What shall we do?
Winkie has no tail."

31

Then with a "Too, too, too!"
and a "Choo, choo, choo!"
away went the Little Tin Train.

It ran back to the toy shop,
and jumped into the box
where it lived.

Richard Wilson, **The foundations of reading**, *Pupil's book B*, London and Edinburgh: Thomas Nelson and Sons, *c*.1929

84 pp, 190 × 140 mm

Illustrations: Cyril Cowell

· A series described on the title page as 'The individual method of learning to read by word and picture matching, phonics and phrasing'.

· Set in 18-point Antique Old Style with tight line spacing and variable word spacing as a result of justified setting.

· Large and small black-and-white illustrations are used throughout; full-page, full-colour illustrations illustrate some of the stories, but the content of the picture does not always relate to the facing text.

But Twirly was sad about the mouse. It had come out at night when the things came alive and it had talked to her.

Ring-o-roses series, *6. Six wee crabs*, London: Cassell and Co, *c*.1929

8 pp, 176 × 135 mm

· One of a series of forty-eight short books 'for use in the Infant School'.

· Set in a 24-point Old Style with no additional space between the lines.

· An unusual feature is the numbering of the paragraphs from 1 on each page.

· Each spread has a coloured illustration.

SIX WEE CRABS.

1. Jim got the crab. It was so big, but it did not let Joe's toe go.

2. Joe had to hop and hop. But still Mama Crab had his toe.

3. "Put the net on the rock," said Joe, "and try to get the crab off."

4. Jim put his net on the rock and the wee crabs in it fell out. The crabs ran and ran to get to the pool.

6

1. Soon the Mama Crab let the toe go, and Jim and Joe fell in the pool.

2. Mama Crab ran off and hid. Jim was so wet. Joe was wet, too, and his toe was bad.
"Let us go," said Joe to Jim.

7

SIX WEE CRABS.

1. Mama Crab saw Jim and Joe put the six crabs in the net. She was so sad, but she said, "I will get my crabs if I can." She hid in a pool.

2. Jim and Joe saw the pool. "Let us go in the pool," said Joe; "I am so hot. It will be cool in the pool." So into the pool he ran; Jim ran in, too.

3. "Ha! Ha!" said Mama Crab. "I will get you. I will get you." She ran to Joe and bit his big toe.

4

1. "O! O! O!
A crab has my toe
It will not let go,"
said Joe. He *did* yell!

2. Jim ran to Joe! The Mama Crab had the end of his toe. It was so red.

3. "I will get the crab off," said Jim.

5

3. "Ha! Ha!" said Mama Crab. "I will get you. I will get you." She ran to Joe and bit his big toe.

The Seandar individual reading books, *My first reading book*, Leeds: E.J. Arnold & Son, *c.*1929

12 pp, 183 × 139 mm

- This series was first published as 'The "Seandar" individual reading books' by Cartwright and Rattray, Educational Publishers, Hyde, Cheshire and then by E.J. Arnold & Son of Leeds. In the 1930s the same books were published as 'The individual reading books'.

- The first two books in this series use a handwritten form described by the publishers as 'White Script Letters'. Some kind of stencil may have been used for character assembly. The third book in the series is set in Gill Sans.

- The word spacing is variable and sometimes reduced to make the words fit the line.

- According the comment on the back cover of the Cartwright and Rattray edition of one of the 'Reading and writing booklets' the illustrations in the reading books 'have been specially drawn for them by a first-class Artist. An illustration appears on practically every page and the pictures have been designed and coloured in a full range of colours to appeal to the children and keep them interested throughout the series'.

I. Lang, **The "Seandar" reading and writing booklets. Set B2**, *Birds*, Hyde: Cartwright & Rattray Ltd, *c*.1929, 8 pp, 183 × 139 mm

· This was a companion series to the 'Seandar individual reading books', using the same handwritten letterforms:
'The sentences are in script letters, and the clever silhouette pictures are a special feature. Each booklet has six pages, printed on thick green paper of pleasing shade and hard wearing quality'.

· The black silhouette illustrations are less appealing than those in the reading books.

Book design for children's reading

Jane Brown, **The radiant way**, *First step*, Edinburgh and London: W. & R. Chambers, 1933

Illustrations: Rene Cloke

40 pp, 196 × 148 mm

- A series of four books first published in 1933 that combines phonic and sentence methods. The Preface lists the 'distinguishing features' of the book, including
  – 'Look-and-say' words ... printed in distinctive type at the top of each lesson.'
  – 'Exclamation marks have been deliberately excluded as tending to add to the difficulties of the young reader'.

- Typeset in 24-point Monotype Imprint 101 with wide word spacing and a variable line length determined to some extent by the positioning of the pictures.

- Paragraphs are numbered with the first line extended to the left, a convention widely used at the end of the nineteenth century.

- Small coloured illustrations are used throughout the text; the type is often re-arranged to fit around them.

Revisal

Mother sing to come Ann
for Thank you the dance
will show Bring see

1. Mother has a rod for Pat.
2. Thank you, Mother, for the rod.
3. Pat, show the rod to Ann.
4. Mother has not a rod for Ann.
5. Mother has a pad for Ann.
6. Thank you, Mother, for the pad.
7. Ann will show the pad to Pat.

14

Father

1. Father has a top for Pat.
2. Father has a fan for Ann.
3. Father and Mother show the top to Pat.
4. Father and Mother show the fan to Ann.
5. Come for the top, Pat.
6. Come for the fan, Ann.
7. Pat and Ann ran for the top and the fan.

15

PHONIC DRILL

a n c p s t h d

h	ha	hat
t	ta	tap
c	ca	cap
c	ca	cat
p	pa	pan
P	Pa	Pat

'SOUND-AND-SAY' WORDS

sat has can
had nap and
at as an

6

Mother sing to

1. Sing. Sing. Sing.
2. Sing, Mother, sing.
3. Can Mother sing?
4. Mother can sing.
5. Pat can sing.
6. Pat, sing to Mother.
7. Sing to Pat, Mother.

7

1. Father has a top for
2. Father has a fan for
3. Father and Mother show the top to Pat.
4. Father and Mother show the fan to Ann
5. Come for the top, Pa

Donalda Mackay, **The London supplementary readers**, *A7*. *The runaway kite*, London: University of London Press, 1937

16 pp, 180 × 135 mm

· A book from the first of two series 'for children of 6–8 years'.

· Set in 18-point Plantin, ranged left with tight line spacing.

· An unusual feature is the two-level chapter headings.

· A boxed illustration in black plus orange precedes each short (two pages) chapter.

Some children had pretty kites, like Jess and John.
There were blue kites and green, yellow kites and red.
"I like ours best," Jess said.
"So do I," said John.
"You hold up the kite, Jess. I will run on with the string."
Up went the kite, up and up. It looked like a big red bird.
"Don't let it fly too high, John," Jess said. "It is much higher than that blue kite over there."
"Yes. It is highest of all."
"Let me hold the string," said Jess. The kite went higher and higher.
"Oh, look!" said Jess.
"Give me the string," said John.
"It will bump that yellow one." But John was too late.

10

Chapter 6
THE RUNAWAY KITE
The kites did not bump after all, but the strings got crossed.
"Look out!" said Jess.
"The string of the yellow kite will saw our string in two. Quick! Pull it away, John."
"I am trying to," John said, "but it will not come. Oh, dear!"

11

"I heard him singing in his bath. Mother says he has a surprise for us."
John ran back to his room. Jess jumped out of bed quickly. She was soon ready.
They ran quickly down the stairs to meet Uncle Jim.
"Good morning, Uncle Jim."
"Good morning. I think I know why you are up early this morning." Uncle Jim smiled. "Here it is."
"What a big parcel!" John said.
"What is in it?" Jess asked.
"Look and see," said Uncle Jim. They took the paper off quickly. Under that there was more paper.
"Oh!" said John.
"Oh!" said Jess.
"A red kite!"
"Thank you very much, Uncle Jim."

4

Chapter 3
NO FLYING TO-DAY
The children were very pleased with Uncle Jim's surprise.
"Can you fly kites?" he asked.
"Oh, yes, Uncle Jim," they said.
"Will you come out with us?"
"Yes, I will, but not to-day, I think. It looks like rain."

5

Some children had pretty kites, like Jess and John.
There were blue kites and green, yellow kites and red.

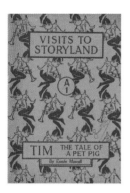

Esmée Mascall, **Visits to storyland**, *Tim, the tale of a pet pig*, London: McDougall's Educational Co, 1930s

16 pp, 196 × 136 mm

· From the inside front cover: 'A delightful new series of supplementary readers characterised by charming stories, beautiful illustrations and handsome production.' This is the first of the series: 'for ages 5, 6'.

· Set justified in 24-point Imprint 101.

· Two-colour illustrations are used throughout in a variety of formats including extending across the centre spread.

Down went the man! Down went the pail! All the milk was spilt in the yard.

The man hurt his leg and had to rub it hard. Tim saw that he was very cross.

8

"Just you wait till I get you!" said the man.

But Tim did not wait. The yard gate was not shut, so he ran out of the yard.

Then he had a peep at the man from a hole in

9

4

CHAPTER 2

One day Tim woke up to hear the rain fall pit-a-pat on the roof. He felt cross.

"I hate a wet day," said Tim.

Then he saw Ann's face at the gate of his sty.

"Tig-tig! Come out and eat your meal, Tim!" said Ann.

"No, I will not!" said the bad pig, and he lay still.

But when he saw Ann go, he came out.

5

"Just you wait till I get you!" said the man.
But Tim did not wait.
The yard gate was not

Fannie Wyche Dunn, Franklin T. Baker, Ashley H. Thorndike, **New everyday classics**, *Primer: part II*, London: Macmillan and Co, 1935

Illustrations: Maud and Miska Petersham

112 pp, 185 × 130 mm

· A series first published by Macmillan in New York in 1926.

· Set in an 18-point modern-face type with a bold slab serif for headings.

· As other reading books that originated in the United States, even word spacing and generous space between the lines results in a light and airy page.

· Distinctive illustrations show clever use of black plus two colours.

Jack and Jill

Jack and Jill
Went up the hill
To get a pail of water.
Jack fell down
And broke his crown,
And Jill came tumbling after.

70

Two Little Blackbirds

Two little blackbirds
Sitting on a hill,
This one is Jack,
That one is Jill.
Fly away, Jack.
Fly away, Jill.
Come back, Jack.
Come back, Jill.

71

" Well, that is just what I will do,"
said Mr. Man.
So he threw Mr. Rabbit
right into the middle of the briars.
Then Mr. Rabbit jumped up.
" Mr. Man, Mr. Man," he called,
" I live in the briars, Mr. Man."
And Mr. Rabbit ran away.

82

Read and Do

1. Go to the door.
2. Put your hand on the door.
3. Run and shut the door.
4. Draw a big apple.
5. Make the apple red.
6. Sit down by somebody.
7. Sit down by a boy.
8. Play you are milking a cow.
9. Play you are throwing a stone.
10. Play you are blowing a feather.
11. Play you are jumping over a wall.
12. Play you are making a fire.
13. Play you are tasting soup.

83

1. Go to the door.

2. Put your hand on the door.

3. Run and shut the door.

4. Draw a big apple.

5. Make the apple red.

Ellen Ashley, **The John and Mary readers**, *John and Mary's toys*, Huddersfield: Schofield & Sims, 1930s

Illustrations: E. L. Turner

44 pp, 180 × 135 mm

· A series of four books: *Introductory book*, *Book 1*, *Book 2*, *Book 3*, supplemented later by an *Intermediate book* (shown here) between the *Introductory book* and *Book 1*.

· The series was 'planned to carry out the "Sentence Method" of teaching reading, and is the result of much careful experiment.'

· Typeset in 24-point Granby.

· Illustrated with distinctive black and white linocuts.

The Peg family first readers,
1. The home, London: Macmillan
and Co, 1935

16 pp, 185 × 153 mm

· This is described on the back cover
  as 'A progressive series of three
  First readers, written in well-spaced
  SCRIPT PRINT, with each sentence
  illustrated by a PEG FIGURE.'

· Set in a grot with modified 'a' and
  'g' with wide word spacing, though
  some longer lines are made to fit by
  slightly reducing it.

· Prominence is given to the page
  numbers which are set in the same
  size as the text.

· Each line of text is illustrated
  with unusual small drawings of
  members of the Peg family.

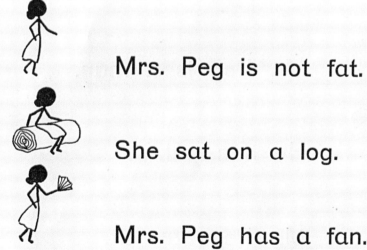

Belle Rose, **Wheaton's rhythmic readers**, *Book two*, Exeter: A. Wheaton & Co, 1938
Illustrations: W. Lindsay Cable
56 pp, 209 × 133 mm

· A series that promoted the 'word approach' to the teaching of reading, 'otherwise children are apt to halt their reading progress for the sake of word analysis'.

· Set in 18-point Rockwell Light with variable letter spacing.

· Word spacing is even and lines are short. On a few occasions the letter-spacing, rather than the word spacing, is reduced to make a line fit the measure.

· The space between the lines is reduced on some pages so that the text fits.

· A distinctive feature is the brightly coloured illustrations which use a solid bright green, red, yellow and blue and tints of these colours.

Page 24   LESSON 20.

Can you dance little girl,
Can you dance with me ?
Yes I can dance
As you well can see.

Can you sing little girl,
Can you sing low and high ?
Yes I can sing,
Like a lark in the sky

Page 25

Can you whistle little boy,
Can you whistle like me ?
Yes I can whistle
Like a bird in the tree.

Can you swim little boy,
Can you swim like me ?
Yes I can swim
Like a fish in the sea.

Page 16   LESSON 14.

Kitty cat is in the garden.
Kitty cat is my pussy.
She sees Tom-tit.
Tom-tit is a little bird.
He is up in the tree.
"Come to me," says Kitty cat.
Tom-tit is very wise.
"No thank you," he says.

Page 17

"I shall not come to you.
"I shall not fly to you.
"I shall not come near you.
"Your claws are too sharp.
"Your teeth are too strong.
"Go away Kitty cat. Go away."

"Sit by me," says Kitty cat.
Tom-tit was very wise.
"No thank you," he says.
"I do not like you, Kitty cat,
"I think you want to eat me."
Pussy says, "Mew-mew."
"I do want to eat you.
"I wish I could catch you now."

Can you dance little girl,
Can you dance with me ?
Yes I can dance
As you well can see.

From 1915 to the 1930s

Ellen Ashley, **The Mac and Tosh readers**, *Mac and Tosh play games*, Huddersfield: Schofield and Sims, *c.*1938
Illustrations: Rita Townsend
48 pp, 184 × 138 mm

· A series of many books produced from the end of the 1930s. It was characterised by clear typography, and simple illustrations using flat colours. The first books in the series were typeset in Granby, the later ones in Gill Sans.

· *Mac and Tosh play games*, shown here, is set in 24-point Granby.

· The typography is inconsistent. On some of the pages the text is ranged left, on others it is centred, and sometimes centred and ranged left text appears in the same paragraph.

· Lines of text are, for the most part, very short and some account has been taken of meaning in relation to line breaks.

Jim looked
at the things
on his desk.

18

Page from Ellen Ashley, 'The Mac and Tosh
readers', *Mac and Tosh go to school*, illustrated by
Rita Townsend, *c.*1938

Eila Mackenzie, **Simple reading steps**, *Step 7. The red fairy*, Glasgow and London: House of Grant, 1930s

12 pp, 193 × 151 mm

Illustrations: Margaret Tarrant

· A series of over 40 short books published from the 1930s to the 1950s. Eila Mackenzie and Margaret Tarrant worked on books 1–12.

· The typeface used is the same as that used in 'The songs the letters sing', also published by Grant in the 1920s (see p.99).

· Justified setting without word breaks results in very uneven word spacing.

· Paragraphs are shown by a very large indent plus additional space.

· Lists of words that appear in each chapter are given at the beginning.

One day a little
moon fairy got out of bed
as soon as it began to get
dark. He came down
from the pale sky, and
went hop, hop, on the sea,

Step 12

Page from Eila Mackenzie, 'Simple reading
steps', *Step 12. The moon fairy*, illustrated by
Margaret Tarrant, 1930s

Jane Brown, **The new star infant readers**, *Book one*, Glasgow: Robert Gibson & Sons, 1940

Illustrations: Irene Mountfort

40 pp, 190 × 140 mm

· The first of a series of four books described in the preface as follows: 'This new series of Infant Books is based on a combination of the Phonic and Sentence Methods of teaching Reading, and provides a scheme whereby accurate and intelligent reading can be obtained.'

· The typography and use of illustrations is similar to that in 'The radiant way' (by the same author).

· Typeset in 24-point Baskerville with wide word spacing and a variable line length determined by the position of the pictures. The Preface notes that one of the 'main features' is the exclusion of exclamation marks to avoid distraction' (as was the case in 'The radiant way').

· Paragraphs are numbered with the first line extended to the left, a convention typical at the end of the nineteenth century.

· Full-colour illustrations are used throughout.

Frances Roe, **Fundamental reading**, *A2. Christmas*, Bickley: University of London Press, 1944

16 pp, 194 × 138 mm

· One of a series of graded readers: A to D. The D series is for more experienced readers; the type is smaller and the stories are longer.

· Typeset in a version of Caslon Bold.

· Although the type is ranged left, the word spacing is variable as is the line spacing.

· Illustrations in black plus blue or orange are positioned consistently above the text on each page.

Tommy sits up in his little cot.

"Has Father Christmas come, Jack?"

"Get your stocking and see."

Tommy gets it as fast as he can.
Father Christmas has come.
His stocking is as fat as can be.

It has lots of toys in it.
Some are big, some are small.

At the top is a big red balloon.

2

Tommy is a happy boy.
Jack and Jill are happy, too.
They like Christmas stockings.

"May we get up, Mother?"

"Yes, you may if you like."

"Come on, Tommy. I will help you."

Jill helps Tommy to dress.
Then they run down-stairs.

Tommy still has his red balloon.

3

Tommy has a little toy bear.
It goes over and over and over.

"I think Wagger will like that.
Wagger, come and see Tommy's bear."

Wagger comes to look at it.

She thinks, "What can this be?"

The little bear goes over and over.

Wagger runs as fast as she can.
She does not like the little bear.

8

Tommy has a big box of wood bricks.
Some are white and some are blue.
They are made of wood.

Jill helps Tommy with his bricks.

"What shall we make, Tommy?"

"Let us make a little house."

Jack helps Tommy to make
a little house with his bricks.

It has a door and six windows.

9

Tommy gets it as fast as he can.
Father Christmas has come.
His stocking is as fat as can be.

It has lots of toys in it.
Some are big, some are small.

The 1940s and 1950s

Hilda Haig-Brown and Zillah Walthew, **The romance of reading infant series**, *Book 2. At the shops*, Oxford: Oxford University Press, 1943

Illustrations: Marcia Lane Foster and Dudley Jarrett

48 pp, 189 × 145 mm

· A series of four books, accompanied by four related 'Play books'. The series promoted the sentence method of teaching to read and was 'designed to meet the needs of children during their first two years at school, that is, from the age of about five to seven plus'. (*Teacher's book*, p.3)

· Set in 24-point Grot 51 with infant characters. The *Teacher's book* notes: 'The whole series is printed in SCRIPT WRITING, based on the straight line and the circle, so that children may copy from their reading books with advantage, and the learning of reading and writing may proceed at the same time.' (p.5).

· The use of red for rhymes is a distinctive feature, and throughout the book there are pages where the type has been incorporated into the picture, as in this example of a cat.

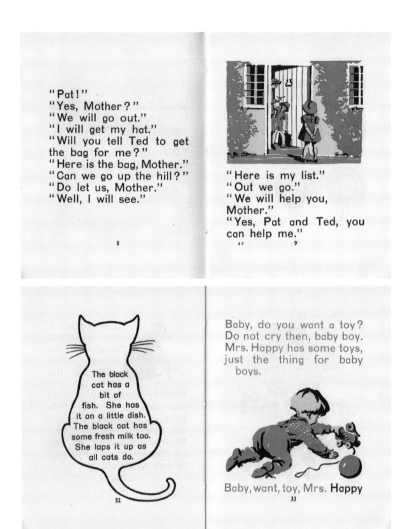

"Pat!"
"Yes, Mother?"
"We will go out."
"I will get my hat."
"Will you tell Ted to get the bag for me?"
"Here is the bag, Mother."
"Can we go up the hill?"
"Do let us, Mother."
"Well, I will see."

8

"Here is my list."
"Out we go."
"We will help you, Mother."
"Yes, Pat and Ted, you can help me."

9

The black cat has a bit of fish. She has it on a little dish. The black cat has some fresh milk too. She laps it up as all cats do.

32

Baby, do you want a toy? Do not cry then, baby boy. Mrs. Happy has some toys, just the thing for baby boys.

Baby, want, toy, Mrs. Happy

33

"I will get my hat."
"Will you tell Ted to get the bag for me?"
"Here is the bag, Mother."
"Can we go up the hill?"
"Do let us, Mother."
"Well, I will see."

Book design for children's reading

Page from Hilda Haig-Brown and Zillah
Walthew, 'The romance of reading infant series',
Playbook 1, illustrated by Marcia Lane Foster
and Dudley Jarrett, 1943

Fred Schonell and Irene Serjeant, **The happy venture readers**, Edinburgh and London: Oliver and Boyd, c.1945–

A scheme that combines phonic and sentence methods. It comprises an introductory book, four main ones and 'Playbooks' and 'Library books' designed to relate to the main books. It is one of the first schemes where the typeface is used to denote progression: sanserif type (Gill Sans) is used for the introductory stages to align with handwritten letterforms, and serif type (Century Schoolbook) as the scheme progressed.

In all the books turn-over lines are indented and broken according to meaning.

The *Introductory book* is set in 24 point Gill Sans, ranged left with wide word spacing.

The scheme ran to numerous editions, published until the 1970s. Though the illustrations were revised, other aspects of visual organisation remain the same.

Fred Schonell and Irene Serjeant, **The happy venture readers**, *Introductory book. Fluff and Nip*, c.1945
Illustrations: C.J. McCall
24 pp, 194 × 145 mm

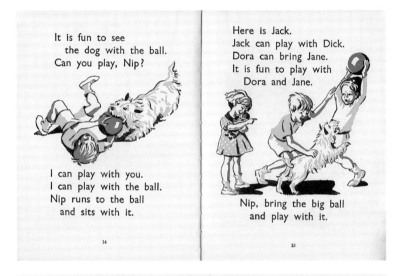

Fred Schonell and Phyllis Flowerdew, **Happy venture library**, *Book 1. Pig*, c.1950
10 pp, 137 × 151 mm

Fred Schonell and Irene Serjeant, **The happy venture readers**, *Book one. Playtime*, c.1945

Illustrations: C.J. McCall

48 pp, 194 × 145 mm

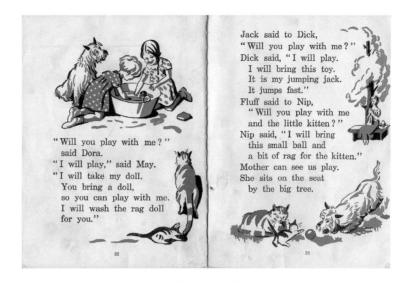

"Will you play with me?" said Dora.
"I will play," said May.
"I will take my doll.
You bring a doll,
so you can play with me.
I will wash the rag doll
for you."

Jack said to Dick,
"Will you play with me?"
Dick said, "I will play.
I will bring this toy.
It is my jumping jack.
It jumps fast."
Fluff said to Nip,
"Will you play with me
and the little kitten?"
Nip said, "I will bring
this small ball and
a bit of rag for the kitten."
Mother can see us play.
She sits on the seat
by the big tree.

32   33

Nip said, "I will bring
this small ball and
a bit of rag for the kitten.
Mother can see us play.

Fred Schonell and Phyllis Flowerdew, **Happy venture**, *Playbook 3. Now for some stories*, 1971 edn (first published 1954)

Illustrations: Jack Keay and William Semple

92 pp, 215 × 138 mm

· In this 1971 edition the content and typography remain the same as in the 1954 one. The name of the scheme is shortened to 'Happy venture', the illustrations and cover are updated.

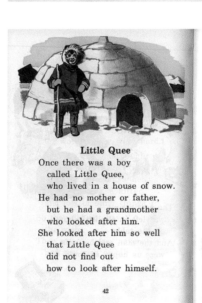

Little Quee
Once there was a boy
called Little Quee,
who lived in a house of snow.
He had no mother or father,
but he had a grandmother
who looked after him.
She looked after him so well
that Little Quee
did not find out
how to look after himself.

42

When he wanted something,
Grandmother was there
to give it to him.
When he fell over,
Grandmother was there
to help him up,
and Little Quee
did not find out
how to look after himself.
But one day
Grandmother had a bad leg,
and could not walk.
She could only
hop to the door
of the house of snow.
She could only
sit in the sun
and look at Little Quee.

43

Book design for children's reading

E. G. Hume, **The happy way to reading**, *Introductory book*, Glasgow and London: Blackie and Son, 1946

32 pp, 187×137 mm

· A set of five reading books that combined the 'direct' approach to reading with 'systematic work in phonics.' A feature of the scheme was that its carefully controlled vocabulary meant that it used more words than usual in the first stages because 'too small a vocabulary tends to artificiality of form, poverty of ideas, and a too wearisome repetition.'

· Book 1 is set in 24-point Gill Sans, ranged left typesetting with wide word spacing and short lines.

· Turn-over lines are indented with lines broken according to meaning.

· A distinctive illustrative style exploits the tonal range achieved through use of red and green in addition to black.

· From *Book two* the text is set in Imprint 101 with less space between the words than in *Book one*, but with generous space between the relatively short lines.

Father is very busy
in the garden.
What is he doing?
Tom is busy, too.
What is he doing?

24

Baby Ann is in bed.
Tom and Joan will soon be
in bed, too.

25

Here you see all the family.
It is a happy family.

6

Ann has a doll.
Joan has a doll.
Tom has a ball.
Mother has Ann
in her arms.
Father has hold of
Joan's hand.
They are all going off
to the park.

(c06)   7   A2

Father is very busy
in the garden.
What is he doing?

Ella Ruth Boyce, **Activity reading scheme**, *My first story book*, London: Macmillan and Co, 1940s [1950 reprint]

32 pp, 189 × 135 mm

· A series comprising a primer and three readers plus 'The little books': graded readers to follow the 'story books'.

· Typeset in 24-point Gill Sans with infant 'a' and 'g', ranged left with wide word spacing and short lines.

· Additional vertical space is inserted between each group of two lines of text.

· The use of cut-out illustrations increases the amount of space on the page.

Jim is in his car.
It is big and green.

I will put my car
here, said Jim.

6

Mothers and Fathers.

Ann is the mother.
She is a girl.

Jim is the father.
He is a boy.

7

Here we go in
father's big car.
Baby likes to go
with father.

The car will go
to the red house.
Here, mother.
Here we are.

10

The Letter.

Jim said, Do come
and play with me.
I am a boy. I will be
the postman.

You are a girl.
Will you be
the mother?
Bath the baby and
put her to bed, please.

11

I will put my car
here, said Jim.

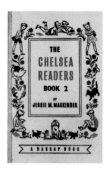

Jessie Mackinder, **The Chelsea readers**, *Book 2*, London: George Harrap & Co, 1946

48 pp, 215 × 140 mm

- A series of five books intended to be read progressively and where the use of red as a second colour is used to direct the reader. Red page numbers denote class lessons; black page numbers indicate those to be read by children on their own.

- Unusually for a reading book published in the 1940s, each of the books in the series increases in difficulty throughout with more text on the later pages in the book.

- Reminiscent of the reading books produced at the end of the nineteenth century, the book begins with an illustrated alphabet.

- Typeset in Perpetua.

- Small illustrations printed in black, orange and red are placed in different positions throughout the book.

6

 1. Ben ran and Tom ran.

 2. He fell.

 3. The big top hat fell off.

 4. It fell into the mud.

 5. The red cap did not.

 6. Ben ran to Tom.

7. The big hat has mud on it.

 8. The red cap has not got mud on it.

Lesson 7

7

by   was

 1. A hat-peg.

2. The six hat-pegs.

 3. Ben's cap was on a peg.

4. Tom's hat was by Ben's cap.

 5. Tom was by a bus.

6. Ben was by Tom.

7. The bus was big.

8. Tom was not big.

Lesson 8

18

Dad said, "I must get a best hat for you, Ben."

Ben said, "I am big. Will you get a man's hat for me, Dad?"

Dad said, "I will get a man's hat for you, Ben."

Tom said, "Will you get a man's hat for me, Dad?"

Dad said, "I will not get a red cap for you; I will get a man's hat for best."

You can see the men's hats Dad got for Ben and Tom for best.

Lesson 14

19

Jill is six.

Nan is not as big as Jill.

Nan is not six.

Dad said, "I will get a best hat for Jill and a best bon-net for Nan."

Jill said, "Will you get a red hat for me, Dad?"

"I will if I can," said Dad.

Dad did get a red hat. It had red ribbon on it.

Lesson 15

Dad said, "I will not get a red cap for you; I will get a man's hat for best."

Book design for children's reading

Evans activity readers,
Out to play, London: Evans Brothers, 1947

Illustrations: Audrey Brunton

32 pp, 187 × 124 mm

· A series where the titles reflect everyday activities that children would be familiar with, such as *Washing* and *Pets*.

· Set in 18-point Gill Sans Bold justified with additional space at sentence ends and tight line spacing.

· Full-colour illustrations are used throughout. They were described in the *National Froebel Bulletin* in 1950: 'the illustrations convey in a quite remarkable manner a sense of real children doing real things.'

· Unusually there are no navigation devices, such as page numbers or headings.

"Let's go to the shop and buy one," said Richard.

In the shop window were yellow tops, red tops, green tops and blue tops. There were big tops and little tops and peg tops, too, and whips of all colours to match them.

"How much money have you got?" said Richard.

As Margaret counted her money she said: "I've got sixpence and a penny and a half-penny, too. Is that enough?"

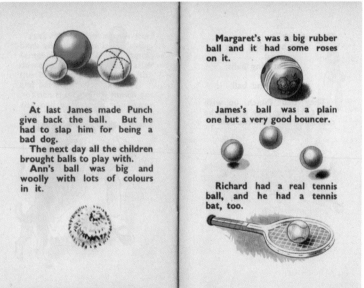

At last James made Punch give back the ball. But he had to slap him for being a bad dog.

The next day all the children brought balls to play with.

Ann's ball was big and woolly with lots of colours in it.

Margaret's was a big rubber ball and it had some roses on it.

James's ball was a plain one but a very good bouncer.

Richard had a real tennis ball, and he had a tennis bat, too.

In the shop window were yellow tops, red tops, green tops and blue tops. There were big tops and little tops and peg tops, too, and whips of all colours to match them.

The 1940s and 1950s

Mabel O'Donnell and Rona Munro, **The Janet and John books**, London: James Nisbet & Co, 1949/1950s

The Janet and John scheme was first published as 'Alice and Jerry' in the United States before being licensed by Nisbet and anglicised.

It comprises two different sets of books that use almost identical pictures and stories; one set with five titles: *Off to play*, *Out and about*, *I went walking*, *Through the garden gate* and *I know a story* use the 'look and say' method; the other set *Janet and John Books 1–4* have a phonic basis. 'My little books' supplement the early books in the scheme and 'The story books' the more advanced books.

Century Schoolbook is used throughout the scheme, though in the 1960s i.t.a. and print-script editions were produced.

Mabel O'Donnell and Rona Munro, **The Janet and John books**, *Out and about*, 1949–
Illustrations: Florence and Margaret Hoopes
40 pp, 198 × 138 mm

I see something.
I see something brown.
It is a brown dog.
Look, little dog.

Let us go home.
Come home, Janet.
Come home, little dog.

Mabel O'Donnell and Rona Munro, **The Janet and John books**, *Book two*, 1949–
Illustrations: Florence and Margaret Hoopes
54 pp, 198 × 138 mm

· Janet and John *Book 2* gives lists of new words in bold type above the text in which they first appeared.

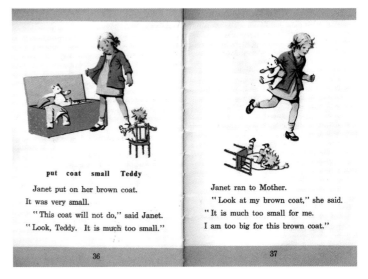

put   coat   small   Teddy
Janet put on her brown coat.
It was very small.
"This coat will not do," said Janet.
"Look, Teddy. It is much too small."

Janet ran to Mother.
"Look at my brown coat," she said.
"It is much too small for me.
I am too big for this brown coat."

Mabel O'Donnell and Rona Munro, **The Janet and John books**, *Book three*, 1950
Illustrations: Florence and Margaret Hoopes
80 pp, 198 × 138 mm

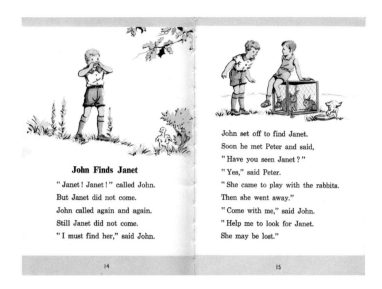

John Finds Janet

"Janet! Janet!" called John.
But Janet did not come.
John called again and again.
Still Janet did not come.
"I must find her," said John.

John set off to find Janet.
Soon he met Peter and said,
"Have you seen Janet?"
"Yes," said Peter.
"She came to play with the rabbits.
Then she went away."
"Come with me," said John.
"Help me to look for Janet.
She may be lost."

Miriam Huber, Frank Salisbury and Mabel O'Donnell, **The Janet and John story books**, *No. 27. The lion and the mouse*, 1951
Illustrations: Mary Royt
24 pp, 195 × 134 mm

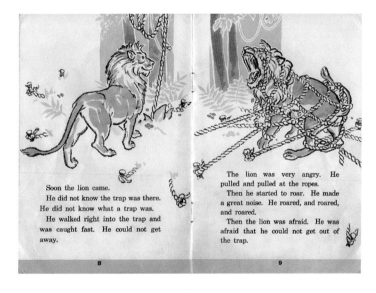

Soon the lion came.
He did not know the trap was there.
He did not know what a trap was.
He walked right into the trap and was caught fast. He could not get away.

The lion was very angry. He pulled and pulled at the ropes.
Then he started to roar. He made a great noise. He roared, and roared, and roared.
Then the lion was afraid. He was afraid that he could not get out of the trap.

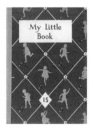

Mabel O'Donnell and Rona Munro, **The Janet and John books**, *My little book. 15*, 1952
Illustrations: Florence and Margaret Hoopes
16 pp, 134 × 97 mm

It was Mother.
Mother came out.
She held a basket.
"You may come, Janet,"
said Mother.
"You may come with me."

The 1940s and 1950s

The 1940s and 1950s

Ella Ruth Boyce, **The gay
way**, *The blue book*, London:
Macmillan & Co, 1950
Illustrations: Lilian Chivers
64 pp, 201 × 150 mm

- A comprehensive graded reading
  scheme comprising a set of six
  graded readers; a set of eight
  stories supplementary to the
  readers, and related apparatus
  such as a picture dictionary and a
  song book.

- *The blue book* is set in 18-point Gill
  Sans with wide word spaces. The
  more advanced books are set in
  Perpetua. The turn-over lines are
  indented and broken in sensible
  places.

- Additional vertical space has been
  inserted between each sentence or
  sentence group suggesting thought
  may have been given to the needs of
  beginner readers.

- The book is printed in black plus
  two spot colours, red and blue,
  which alternate throughout the
  book.

- There are one or two pictures per
  spread that are placed in different
  positions throughout the book.

Ella Ruth Boyce, **The gay
way**, *Blue stories. The black
piglet*, 1958
16 pp, 90 × 123 mm

The dog and the cock
went on and on and on.

Run back to me, said Ken.

The dog and the cock
went on and on and on.

Then the fox ran out of the trees
with his sack.

40

I will have you, cock, he said.

My feathers! said the cock.
The fox will get me.

Run back to me, said Ken.
Then the fox cannot get you.

The dog said, Stop, cock!
Let us run back to the garden
with Ken.

41

A rabbit looked out of the house.
Who are you? she said.

I am a lost baby rabbit.
I ran a long way today,
  and I have lost my way.
I cannot get back to my mother.
Am I your baby rabbit? he said.

No, your legs are too long.
My baby rabbit is not lost,
  she said. He is asleep.

You must go back by the road
  into the garden and up the hill.
Your mother lives up on the hill.
She lives under the old oak tree.

Thank you, said the baby rabbit.
26

Hoppitty-hop, hop,
  skippitty-skip, skip.
Hop, hop, hop, skip, skip.
Run, run, run, run, run
  down the road
  into the garden.
Hop, hop, hop, hop
  up the hill
  to the oak tree.

The dog and the cock
went on and on and on.

But Piglet did not go with her.
He got up on his back legs
  to look out of the window.

I will not go to sleep, he said.
I will not have a rest.
I will go out in the rain.
But the door is shut.

6   7

Some of the children have pennies in their purses.   Some have pennies in their pockets. Some hold pennies in their hands.   One small girl has a silver sixpence in her bag.

The ice-cream man comes nearer and nearer. He pushes his gay ice-cream cart along with him.   The children can see the green and pink and gold cart.   They can hear the gay silver bells as they tinkle.

Page from Ella Ruth Boyce, 'The gay way', *The orange book*, illustrated by Lilian Chivers, 1950

The 1940s and 1950s

J.C. Daniels and Hunter Diack,
The royal road readers,
Book one, part I, London: Chatto
and Windus, 1954
Illustrations: Biro

'The royal road readers' comprises a 'main course' with a series of 'supplementary readers'. The large format *Book one* presents a step-by-step approach beginning with the learning of individual 3-letter words; a second stage of 'letter analysis' introduces children to the idea that letters stand for sounds. By the end of *Book one* children can read short sentences and are introduced to the 'First companion books' to read on their own, and subsequent main books in the series.

Set in Gill Sans with infant 'a' and 'g' throughout. The use of justified setting in *Book two* is unusual in reading books published at this time.

Illustrations are used in a number of ways. In the more advanced books in the series the type sometimes runs around the illustrations.

The 16-page supplementary 'companion books' are of a more conventional reading book format, with large illustrations and text below.

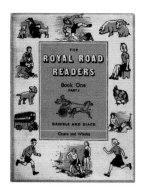

J.C. Daniels and Hunter Diack,
The royal road readers, *Book
one. Part I*, 1954
32 pp, 245 × 186 mm

J.C. Daniels and Hunter Diack,
The royal road readers, *Book
two*, 1954
48 pp, 204 × 140 mm

J.C. Daniels and Hunter Diack,
The royal road readers, 'First
companion books', *5. Rack the
dog*, 1954
16 pp, 176 × 120 mm

Gwen has a pet hen, Bess.

Bess has a nest in a box.

Pat Devenport, **Pilot reading scheme**, Leeds: E. J. Arnold & Son, 1955 [DTC]

A comprehensive scheme comprising four pre-reading books, four 'pilot readers', forty-five 'pilot booklets' and three graded dictionaries. They are described in publicity material as having 'stimulating, brightly-coloured pages'.

Set in a modified version of Gill Sans with infant characters.

Different illustrators are used for different levels within the series.

Pat Devenport, **Pilot reading scheme**, *The toyshop*, 1955
Illustrations: Mary Gernat
32 pp, 188 × 152 mm

We made a toy owl.

22

We made a truck.

23

I can push the truck.

14

I can fly the kite.
I can wash baby clothes.
I can bounce the ball hard.
I can hug the toy rabbit.
I can play with the toy owl.
I can push the truck.

15

I can fly the kite.

I can wash baby clothes.

I can bounce the ball hard.

Pat Devenport, **Pilot reading scheme**, *The train*, 1955
Illustrations: Rosemary Hird
40 pp, 188 × 152 mm

The guard waved to us from his window.

We waved to him.
The signal went up.
It was not green.
It was red.

14

15

We painted our engine red and
we painted our truck

Pat Devenport, **Pilot reading scheme**, *The man and the engine*, c.1955
Illustrations: Pamela Soames
32 pp, 178 × 122 mm

"Oh," said the man.
"Paint Man, will you paint Tractor?
Tractor will not help Farm Man.
Farm Man gave me no hay.
Big Cow gave me no milk.
Signal Man will not put the signal down.
Engine will not go and I cannot go home."

14

15

Pat Devenport, **Pilot reading scheme**, *The baby horse*, c.1955
Illustrations: G. Cattermole
32 pp, 132 × 110 mm

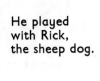

He played with Rick, the sheep dog.

The 1940s and 1950s

Paul McKee, M. Lucile Harrison, Annie McCowen and Elizabeth Lehr, **The McKee readers**, London: Thomas Nelson & Sons, c.1955 [DTC]

A graded reading scheme notable for its teachers' manuals that give page by page instructions for each lesson. The series comprises five staged books, plus twenty-four 'Platform readers' that supplement stages 2–5.

Set in Century Schoolbook in different sizes throughout the series.

The pictures were described as 'the most attractive and lively four-colour illustrations you have seen' in *Child Education*, January 1955.

Paul McKee, M. Lucile Harrison, Annie McCowen and Elizabeth Lehr, **The McKee readers**, *Tip*, c.1955
Illustrations: Corinne Malvern
46 pp, 205 × 148 mm

· Wide word spaces and short sentences that occupy one line suggest consideration of the needs of younger readers.

· The pictures relate to the text on each page, and the idea is that they tell part of the story; on each page there is one large picture and one small one.

Go, Peter.
Find Susan.
Go find Susan

20

Come with me, Susan.
Come home.
Come home with me.

21

No, no! No, Tip!
Go home. Go home.
I will not play with you.
Go home, Tip.

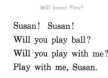

30

Will Susan Play?

Susan! Susan!
Will you play ball?
Will you play with me?
Play with me, Susan.

31

Come home.
Come home with me.

The McKee Platform Readers · B1

Dora Castley, Kathleen Fowler and Sheila Carstairs, **The McKee Platform Readers,** *Something for Kay*, London: Thomas Nelson & Sons, 1958–

Illustrations: Edward W. Robertson

16 pp, 192 × 140 mm

· The 'Platform readers' have a more conventional reading book format with illustrations relevant to the content positioned above the text.

"What can I give to Kay?"
said Penny.
"I have my red ball and my rabbit.
I know!
I will give her my rabbit.
She can do tricks with him.
I will show her a few tricks.
I can make my rabbit hop.
Yes!
I will give my rabbit to Kay."

6

"I know what I can do,"
said Peter.
"Kay wants a fishing net.
I will make one for her.
We can all go to the lake to fish.
Daddy gave me a good fishing net.
I will make one like that for Kay."

7

"Look at the fish near that sand bank,"
said Peter.

"May I try to get one?" asked Penny.

"Yes! Take my net," said Kay.
"Hold the net in that hand.
I will hold this hand.
Now you will not slip."

"You have got one," said Peter.
"Good! Now give the net to Kay."

14

"Look at that big fish," said Susan.
"Try to get it, Kay."

"Yes, try to get that one," said Peter.
"You wanted to get a big fish."

"I have it, I have it!" said Kay.

"Good!" said Peter.
"You are good at fishing, too."

"It was your net that helped me,"
said Kay.

15

"Look at that big fish," said Susan.
"Try to get it, Kay."

"Yes, try to get that one," said Peter.
"You wanted to get a big fish."

"I have it, I have it!" said Kay.

"Good!" said Peter.
"You are good at fishing, too."

Gertrude Kate Dibble, **Playtime books**, *1: Here I am*, London: Thomas Nelson & Sons, *c*.1950

Illustrations: Barbara Gray

16 pp, 188 × 137 mm

· One of a series of twelve beginner readers designed to support 'reading with meaning', such that the content relates to a child's everyday experience.

· The visual characteristics of the series are described in the September 1950 issue of *Child Education*: 'The Playtime books are attractively produced with large clear print and illustrations in colour on every page. They are well bound with pleasantly coloured covers, each book containing 16 pages.'

· Typeset in 24-point Gill Sans with wide word spaces.

· Short sentences occupy one line; occasional turnover lines are indented.

· The pictures relate to the text on each page; they are not positioned consistently from spread to spread.

Here is my doll.
I dress her.
I nurse her.
I push her pram.

8

I put her to bed.

Do you dress your doll?
Do you nurse her?
Do you push her pram?
Do you put her to bed?

Yes, I do.

9

Here is my teddy bear.
I hug him.
I put a hat on him.
I take him for a walk.

10

I take him up to bed.

Do you hug your teddy bear?
Do you put a hat on him?
Do you take him up to bed?
Do you take him for a walk?

Yes, I do.

11

Do you dress your doll?

Do you nurse her?

Do you push her pram?

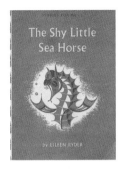

Eileen Ryder, **Stories for me**,
The shy little sea horse, London:
Macmillan & Co, 1959
Illustrations: Esmé Jeudwine
16pp, 185 × 133 mm

· One of a series of six
  'Supplementary readers for infant
  schools with coloured illustrations'.

· Set in 24-point Gill Sans with infant
  characters and generous space
  between the lines.

· Lines are broken according to
  sense.

· The type is printed in dark green
  rather than the usual black which
  provides an additional tonal
  range, along with orange, for the
  illustrations.

· Some illustrations extend across
  both pages of the spread.

But Sam was too shy.
He just shook his head.
Soon he met a lot of crabs.
"Come and play
    with us, Sam,"
    said the crabs.

6

But Sam was too shy.
He just shook his head.
Soon he met a lot of eels.
"Come and play
    with us, Sam,"
    said the eels.

7

But Sam just shook his head.
He wanted to play,
    but he was too shy.
He swam off by himself.

Then he saw
    a little mermaid,
    sitting on the sand.
She was crying.
Sam was very sad
    to see her crying.

9

But Sam just shook his head.
He wanted to play,
    but he was too shy.

Pearl Kettles and Ruby Macdonald, **The vanguard readers**, *First book: Getting ready*, London and Edinburgh: MacDougall's Educational Co, 1950s [DTC]

Illustrations: Cecily Andrews

32 pp, 196 × 138 mm

· A scheme comprising five 'Vanguard Readers' that provides a complete basic course, plus four 'Parallel Readers' and supplementary material in forty-eight 'Vanguard story hour books'. The scheme combines the sentence, look-and-say and phonic methods.

· This appears to be a hand-lettered version of Gill Sans evidenced by variations in same-character shapes. On the page shown (top) the 'm' has been condensed and the space between the letters has been closed up to avoid turnover lines.

· Each sentence begins a new line, resulting in a very ragged right-hand edge.

· The illustrations were described as 'lavish coloured pictures [to] reinforce the impact of the printed word' in the March 1953 issue of *Child Education*, though the range of colours is constrained by the use of just two colours in addition to black.

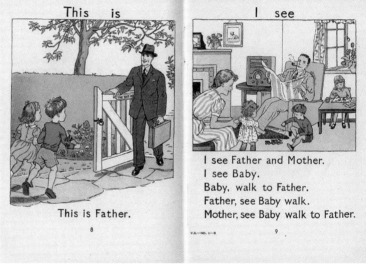

D. G. M. Thomas, **Vanguard parallel readers**, *No. A3. At the market*, London and Edinburgh: MacDougall's Educational Company, 1950s [DTC]

Illustrations: Hilda Boswell

16 pp, 198 × 140 mm

· A series of six books to be read alongside 'The vanguard readers'.

· Typeset in 24-point Baskerville, ranged left with wide word spacing.

· The first line of each paragraph is extended to the left.

· The book begins with a full-page illustration; one or two smaller ones appear on each spread throughout.

· Blue is used throughout as a second colour in the illustrations and for a decorative rule at the foot of each page.

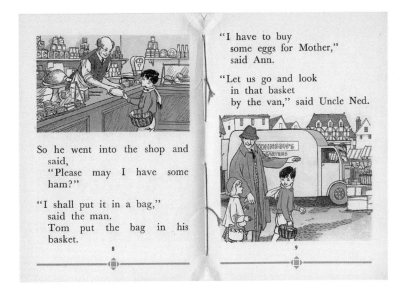

So he went into the shop and said,
  "Please may I have some ham?"

"I shall put it in a bag," said the man.
  Tom put the bag in his basket.

8

"I have to buy
  some eggs for Mother,"
  said Ann.

"Let us go and look
  in that basket
  by the van," said Uncle Ned.

9

4

AT THE MARKET

Tom and Ann
  had come to the market
  with Uncle Ned.

Uncle Ned is a farmer.
  He was to buy a pig.

Ann had to buy
  some eggs for Mother.

Tom had to buy
  some ham for Mother.

Tom had a basket.

Ann had a bag.

"Here are the pigs,"
  said Uncle Ned.
  "Let us buy the pig first."

5

Tom and Ann
  had come to the market
  with Uncle Ned.

Uncle Ned is a farmer.
  He was to buy a pig.

The 1940s and 1950s

Ella Dealtry, **Early steps readers**, *The stream, no. 18*, London: Philip & Tacey, 1954
Illustrated by the author
16pp, 145 × 108 mm

· Typeset in 24-point Futura with wide word spaces. Quotation marks are not used for direct speech.

· Sentences, one or two lines long, are separated by an additional line space.

· In this small-format book the full-page illustrations face the text that relates to them. In the first half of the book the illustrations fall on the left-hand page, and in the second half on the right-hand page, resulting from the imposition of the pages for printing.

What is that? cries Mary to Dick.

She points to a house by the stream.

The stream runs under part of the house.

There is a big wheel by the house.

The wheel is turning.

Mary and Dick make their sticks race.

Soon, the stream comes to a water-fall.

The sticks go over the water-fall.

But Dick's stick gets stuck in some reeds.

The race is over.

What is that? cries
Mary to Dick.

She points to a house
by the stream.

A series of small-format books: 'Blue spot', 'Red spot', 'Green spot' and 'Yellow spot' with appropriately designed covers.

Typeset in a light geometric sanserif that is reminiscent of print-script handwriting models developed in the 1920s.

The type is set with very wide word spaces and seemingly arbitrary indentation of turnover lines.

Mollie Clarke, **Green spot books**, *2: Bear's book of the year*, Exeter: A. Wheaton & Co, *c.*1956 [DTC]
Illustrated by the author
16 pp, 144 × 110 mm

February brings rain.
Bear likes the rain.

March brings wind.
Bear likes the wind.

Mollie Clarke, **Red spot books**, *3: The ducks' pond*, Exeter: A. Wheaton & Co, *c.*1956 [DTC]
Illustrated by the author
16 pp, 144 × 110 mm

But there was a
    fish in the pond.
  He said,
" As sure as I
  Swim by this stone,
  The pond belongs
  To fish alone."

Fish said,
"This pond is for
            fish only

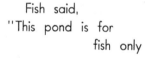

" As sure as I
Swim by this stone,
The pond belongs
To fish alone."

Jenny Taylor and Terry Ingleby,
Let's learn to read, *Book 5. The
Sunday book*, Glasgow: Blackie
& Son, 1960 [DTC]
Illustrations: Gwen Tourret
26 pp, 183 × 140 mm

· A graded scheme of 'red', 'blue'
and 'green' books with progression
within each. It is designed to appeal
to children who live in towns and
cities. One of the main principles of
the scheme is that 'the sense and
the interest of the reading matter
should be the main consideration
and that these should not be
sacrificed to repetition.'

· Set in 24-point Gill Sans with infant
characters and generous space
between the lines.

· Turnover lines are indented.

· Full-colour illustrations in different
positions in relation to the text are
used throughout.

After tea uncle Tom
    takes Carol and Roy
    for a ride in his car.
Roy sits by uncle Tom.
Carol sits at the back.
Off they go.
They go down the street
    past Mrs. Green's shop,
    past the paper shop,
    past the picture house,
    past the letter box,
    past the children's school,
    and back home again.
They have had a lovely ride.

14

15

After dinner mother says,
"Today you may put on
    your new shoes to go
    to Sunday school."
They go upstairs
    and get the new shoes.
Carol puts on
    her red shoes.
Roy puts on
    his brown shoes.
Now they are ready.
The children are so happy.
They like going
    to Sunday school.

10

When they come home
    there is a car
    at the door.

The children run to see
    who has come.
        "Who is it?"
        says Carol.
        "It is aunty May
        and uncle Tom,"
        says Roy.

11

After tea uncle Tom
takes Carol and Roy

Roy and Carol open the door
    and look in the kitchen.
Is the cat in the kitchen?
No.

5

Jenny Taylor and Terry Ingleby,
Let's learn to read, *Little book 1.
The cat*, Glasgow: Blackie & Son,
1960 [DTC]
14 pp, 87 × 133 mm

The 1960s and 1970s

Molly Brearley and Lois Neilson, **Queensway reading**, London: Evans Brothers, 1960s [DTC]

Queensway reading is a vocabulary-based scheme developed from research undertaken at the University of Birmingham. It comprises twenty-six books in six stages, with books in each stage being added later.

The scheme is described in *Child Education*, February 1965: 'the liveliest, most colourful infant reading scheme to appear for a very long time ... based on long and careful research ... supreme in educational value, attractiveness and price.'

Each book is set in Gill Sans in different sizes; infant characters are used in the early books in the scheme.

Molly Brearley and Lois Neilson, **Queensway reading**, *Here we are*, 1964
Illustrations: Peggy Beetles
32 pp, 185 × 125 mm

Molly Brearley and Lois Neilson, **Queensway reading**, *Where are they?*, 1967
Illustrations: Peggy Beetles
32 pp, 185 × 125 mm

"I will go and see what is on the rocks," said Ginger. Soon the boat came up to the rocks. It was lovely there. Ginger looked out at the sea and back at the sand and said, "I like coming out by myself."

But Ginger did not look at the little red boat at all.

The little red boat did not stay by the rocks. It went out on the water for a little way and then a big wave came. The wave pulled the boat away with it, and up and down went the little boat on the water. Away it went out to sea, but Ginger was looking at the waves and the sand.

"Yes, I do like coming out by myself," said Ginger.

6   7

Molly Brearley and Lois Neilson,
Queensway reading, *3b. Let's go to the sea*, 1964
Illustrations: Wendy Marchant
16 pp, 185 × 125 mm

The little red boat did not stay by the rocks. It went out on the water for a little way and then a big wave came. The

Molly Brearley and Lois Neilson,
Queensway reading, *2a. Another day at the station*, 1963
Illustrations: Peggy Beetles
16 pp, 122 × 184 mm

Come along, Robert, says Daddy. You and I are going to the station now.

Is it time for Uncle Jack to come? says Robert.

Yes, says Daddy. The train is coming in soon.

Am I coming? says Judy.

No, says Mummy. You can stay here with me to get the dinner for Uncle. You can make the bed for Uncle, too.

4   5

A.E. Tansley & R.H. Nicholls, **Racing to read**, *Book 1. My house, my garden*, Leeds: E.J. Arnold & Son, 1962

Illustrations: F. Pash

24 pp, 172 × 120 mm

· Typeset in 18-point Gill Sans with infant characters 'a', 'g', 'y', 't'.

· Lines are broken at sentence ends. Longer sentences which turn over are justified resulting in variable word spacing: an example of typesetting convention influencing visual organisation.

· Text is positioned consistently beneath illustrations, or facing illustrations on a double-page spread.

My house has a red roof.
It has a red chimney.
It has a blue window.
It has a blue door.

16

My house has a garden.
It is a big garden.
The garden is big.
The garden of my house is big.

17

This is my house.
It has a red roof and a red chimney.
My house has a blue door.
It has a blue window.
The roof of my house is red and the chimney is red.
The window of my house is blue and the door is blue.
My house has a red roof and a red chimney.
It has a blue door and a blue window.

10

11

My house has a garden.
It is a big garden.
The garden is big.
The garden of my house is big.

Jenny Taylor and Terry Ingleby,
A lot of things, London: Oliver &
Boyd, 1963 [DTC]
20 pp, 140 × 186 mm

An example of the rather extreme
typography used in some reading
schemes published in the 1960s.

She has
a handkerchief
for her nose.

She has
a handkerchief
for her nose.

The Initial Teaching Company was set up to publish books using the Initial Teaching Alphabet with variants of the typeface produced by Monotype.

The impact of the initiative was far reaching and many mainstream educational publishers produced i.t.a. editions of their successful schemes.

John Downing, **The Downing readers**, *Book one. Paul*, London: Initial Teaching Publishing Co, 1963 [DTC]

16 pp, 193 × 143 mm

· Typeset in a semi-bold version of the Initial Teaching Alphabet, ranged left with very wide word spacing.

· Very short lines are broken according to sense.

· The text is positioned consistently beneath the illustrations which are bled-off top, right and left and vignetted at the bottom.

Stuart Bell, **The clearway readers**, *Book one: Tom and Pam*, London: Initial Teaching Publishing Co, 1965 [DTC]

Illustrations: Toni Goffe

16 pp, 210 × 135 mm

- Typeset in the Initial Teaching Alphabet, ranged left with wide word spacing.

- Very short lines are broken according to sense.

- The text is positioned consistently beneath the cut-out illustrations. Red and green, as second colours to highlight the black and white illustrations, are used alternately throughout.

a lam

"a pet lam," seʒ pam.
"a pig!
it iʒ a pig," seʒ tom.
"a pig and a pet lam,"
seʒ pam.

12

tom iʒ on a log.
"ɥied, pam," seʒ tom.
"ɥied, pip," seʒ tom.
tom ɥiedʒ hiʒ ieʒ.

13

pam ɥiedʒ and pip ɥiedʒ.
pam ɥiedʒ in a gap.
pip iʒ not in a gap.
pip ɥiedʒ in a sand pit.

14

a man

it iʒ tom'ʒ dad and pam'ʒ dad.
"it iʒ mie dad," seʒ pam.
"tell tom it iʒ tiem,"
seʒ dad.

15

tom iʒ on a log.
"ɥied, pam," seʒ tom.
"ɥied, pip," seʒ tom.
tom ɥiedʒ hiʒ ieʒ.

James H. Fassett, **The beacon readers**, *At play,* London: Ginn and Company, 1965 (i.t.a. edn) [DTC]

Illustrations: H. Radcliffe Wilson

48 pp, 202 × 134 mm

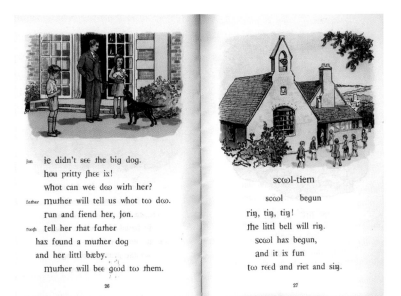

E.S. Bradburne, **Through the rainbow**, *Red book 1,* Huddersfield: Schofield & Sims, 1964 (i.t.a. edn) [DTC]

Photography: F.M. Wilder

32 pp, 247 × 182 mm

E. & W. Bleasdale, **Reading by rainbow**, *Book 2*, Bolton: Moor Platt Press, 1966 [DTC]

Illustrations: Alan Heaps

20 pp, 204×162 mm

· 'Yellow letters are magic i.e. they are not sounded' is one of the principles behind this teacher-inspired scheme. Red is used to denote long vowel sounds, black for letters 'having the usual phonetic sound', and blue for differentiation between 'b' and 'd', and 'o' and 'oo' sounds.

· Typeset in varying sizes of Univers. The different sizes may have been achieved by photographic enlargement of typeset artwork.

tom has a dog.
it is a big dog.
can you see the
    big dog.
up, bob, up.

1

bob is a dog.
tom can run
    and jump.
bob can run.
see tom run and
    hop.

2

i will keep to the path,
said red riding hood.
if i see the big bad wolf
i will run back home.
    the big bad wolf is
hiding in the wood.
    i can see red riding
        hood, he said.

15

red riding hood has
a cake to give to grandma.
    on the way red
riding hood began to
pick some daisies to
give to grandma.
    the big bad wolf
ran on to grandma's
home.
    when he got to
the home he said,
    i will put on grandma's
hat and coat. when
red riding hood comes
she will think i am
grandma.
    red riding hood came
to the home. she
went tap, tap.

16

i will keep to the path,
said red riding hood.
if i see the big bad wolf
i will run back home.
    the big bad wolf is
hiding in the wood.
    i can see red riding

Gertrude Cree, **Getting ready to read**, *Helping mother*, London: Frederick Warne & Co, 1960s
[DTC]
Illustrations: Conrad Frieboe
16 pp, 200 × 140 mm

· Typeset in Gill Sans with infant characters with very wide space between the lines.

· Each right-hand page on the spread is a full-colour illustration.

"Have you a job for me?"

said Mary to Mother.

"Yes," said Mother.

"You can put

the towels

in the cupboard."

"Have you a job for me?"

said Paul to Mother.

"Yes," said Mother.

"You can fill

the wood box."

"Have you a job for me?"

said Mary to Mother.

Cecilia Obrist, **Time for reading**, *Story Book 1. The naughty twins*, London: Ginn and Company, 1967 [DTC]
Illustrations: Douglas Bisset
16 pp, 205 × 137 mm

· A comprehensive scheme in seven stages, devised by teachers. The books come in a range of formats with different styles of illustration including colour photography.

· Most books are set in Plantin with infant characters. Small-format books, such as 'Time for reading quickies' are set in 24-point Gill Sans with infant characters.

· Lines are ranged left with wide word spacing; first lines and direct speech are indented.

· The text is not consistently positioned but arranged around the pictures.

· The use of children's drawings for some of the front covers is a distinctive feature of the scheme.

I tidy the kitchen.

I tidy the sitting-room.

8

In the night Katy and Polly are very, very naughty.

9

In the morning . . . . . this is the kitchen.

What a mess!

10

In the morning . . . . . this is the sitting room.

What a mess!

11

In the night Katy and Polly are very, very naughty.

Cecilia Obrist, **Time for reading quickies**, *Grandpa's book*
Photography: A. Obrist
8 pp, 140 × 100 mm

Grandpa is in his greenhouse.

Grandpa is working here.

Mabel O'Donnell and Rona Munro, **The Kathy and Mark basic readers**, *1 Kathy and Mark*, London and Beccles: James Nisbet & Co, 1970

Illustrations: Beatrice Darwin

32 pp, 210 × 150 mm

· A scheme similar to 'Janet and John', by the same authors.

· Typeset in 24-point Gill Sans Light with infant 'a' and 'g'; an alternative form to the capital 'i' differentiates it from the small letter 'l'.

· The type is ranged left with generous space between words and adequate space between lines.

· The text is positioned above or below the illustrations which are cut out with parts of the image being bled off on many pages.

· This book is divided into four-page sections each preceded by a title in the regular version of the typeface.

Rona Munro and Philippa Murray, **Kathy and Mark**, *Little book. Blue 3*, 1973

8 pp, 145 × 115 mm

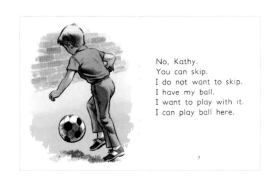

I like this swing.
Two can go on it.
Here we go, Kathy.
We go up and down.
It is a good swing.

16

Page from Mabel O'Donnell and Rona Munro,
'The Kathy and Mark basic readers', *Indoors and
out*, illustrated by Beatrice Darwin, 1970

Dorothy M. Glynn, **Dominoes**, Edinburgh: Oliver & Boyd, 1970s [DTC]

A graded series in six main stages each with six books. 'Dominoes extras' were added later as were related materials including 'chatter cards', film strips, workbooks and games.

Gill Sans with infant 'a' and 'g' was used throughout for the books and the related materials.

The type is ranged left with generous word and line spacing.

Many of the books are illustrated with colour photographs 'designed to encourage observation and language skills.' The bled-off treatment shown here is a distinctive feature of the early stages in the series.

A number of different illustrators are used in the later books in the series.

Dorothy M. Glynn, **Dominoes**, *We go to school*, 1972
Photographs: Eric Johnson
16 pp, 200 × 160 mm

What can we do at school?

bricks

We can play with bricks.

What can we do at school?

Dorothy M. Glynn, **Dominoes**,
Stories about sisters, 1972

Illustrations: Mike Hubbard and
Philip Townsend

32 pp, 200 × 152 mm

· Here, the text is positioned below
the illustrations on most pages,
though is sometimes arranged
around smaller illustrations.

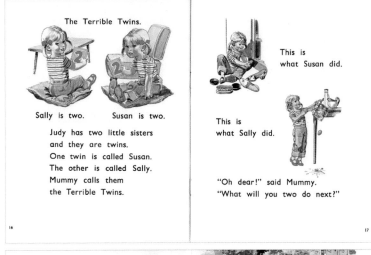

The Terrible Twins.

Sally is two.   Susan is two.

Judy has two little sisters
and they are twins.
One twin is called Susan.
The other is called Sally.
Mummy calls them
the Terrible Twins.

This is
what Susan did.

This is
what Sally did.

"Oh dear!" said Mummy.
"What will you two do next?"

16

17

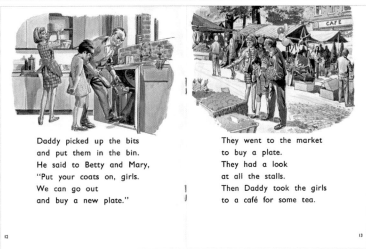

Daddy picked up the bits
and put them in the bin.
He said to Betty and Mary,
"Put your coats on, girls.
We can go out
and buy a new plate."

They went to the market
to buy a plate.
They had a look
at all the stalls.
Then Daddy took the girls
to a café for some tea.

12

13

They went to the market
to buy a plate.
They had a look
at all the stalls.
Then Daddy took the girls
to a café for some tea.

The 1960s and 1970s

Brian Thompson and Pamela Schaub, **Breakthrough to literacy**, *London*: Longman Group, 1970–1980s [DTC]

An approach to early reading and writing based on research at the University of London and supported by the Schools Council. The first twenty-six books in the series were published in 1970 and others were added throughout the 1970s.

Typeset in Gill Sans with infant characters.

The first 'yellow' books have no capital letters other than capital 'I'. The 'red' books use capital letters, but not quotation marks for speech.

The scheme was developed further through the 1970s and 1980s and books continued to be reprinted until well into the 1990s. In the later editions, which include non-fiction and poetry, there is considerable variation in the way that illustrations are used.

David Mackay, Brian Thompson and Pamela Schaub, **Breakthrough to literacy**, *my teacher*, 1970
Illustrations: Janet Alderson
16 pp, 184 × 124 mm

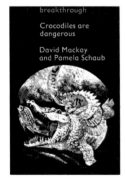

David Mackay and Pamela Schaub, **Breakthrough to literacy**, *Crocodiles are dangerous*, 1972
Illustrations: John Paige
16 pp, 184 × 124 mm

David Mackay, Brian
Thompson and Pamela Schaub,
Breakthrough to literacy,
Spider webs, 1979
Illustrations: John Paige
16 pp, 184 × 124 mm

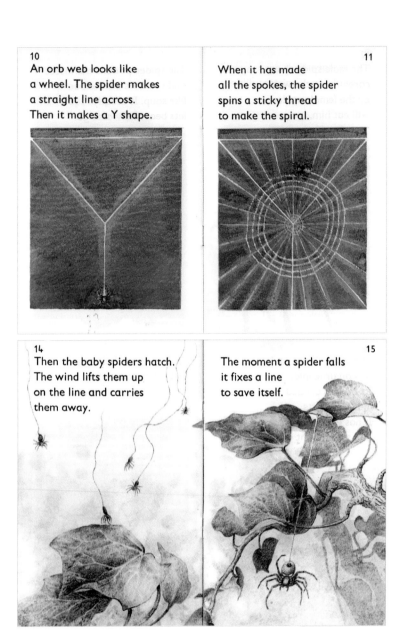

10 An orb web looks like
a wheel. The spider makes
a straight line across.
Then it makes a Y shape.

11 When it has made
all the spokes, the spider
spins a sticky thread
to make the spiral.

14 Then the baby spiders hatch.
The wind lifts them up
on the line and carries
them away.

15 The moment a spider falls
it fixes a line
to save itself.

a wheel. The spider makes
a straight line across.
Then it makes a Y shape.

Jessie Reid and Joan Low, **Link-up build-up**, *Book 1c. My day*, Edinburgh: Holmes McDougall, 1973 [DTC]

Illustrations: Anne Rodger

16 pp, 215 × 170 mm

· Typeset in Optima with infant characters with adequate space between words and lines and ranged-left lines are broken according to sense.

· Capital letters (apart from capital 'I') are not used at the beginning of sentences.

· Text is consistently positioned below the illustrations which are cut out and bled-off in some cases.

I am in school.
I am a policeman
and I am going to the park.

4

my car is a police car.
it is a big car.

5

I met a bus driver today.
the bus was at the bus stop.

12

the driver was going
into the bus
and the bus was going
to the school.

13

the driver was going
into the bus
and the bus was going
to the school.

Rain

R.M. Fisher, M. Hynds, A.M.
Johns, M.G. McKenzie, **Sparks**,
1: Rain, Glasgow and London:
Blackie & Son, 1972 [DTC]
Illustrations: Gareth Floyd
8 pp, 225 × 152 mm

· A series 'to provide an answer to
the constant demand from primary
teachers for books which are
relevant to the lives of children in an
industrial environment'.

· Typeset in an unusual condensed
grot ranged left, with adequate
space between words.

· The space between the lines is
relatively narrow.

· The illustrations take up most
of the page at the expense of the
type, which appears squashed in
beneath the illustrations.

She is all wet.
She falls down in the puddle.
Splash!

She screams and screams.
Mum says, you naughty girl Christine,
and takes her home.

Mum takes Christine to the
supermarket in her pushchair.
Christine wears a big red plastic mac.

Mum goes into the supermarket.
Christine sits by the door.

She is all wet.
She falls down in the puddle.
Splash!

Reading 360: The Ginn reading programme, Aylesbury: Ginn & Company, 1978 [DTC]

This scheme, first published in the US and Australia, comprises a variety of materials to enable teachers to provide a comprehensive language programme for each child – that included reading, listening, speaking and writing.

The Programme is organised in levels and comprises thirty-nine readers and fifty-two 'Magic Circle' books which vary 'in size, shape and presentation and this variation acts as a stimulus to children's interest and motivation'. 'Little books' were added in the 1980s.

The early 'readers' are set in Gill Sans with infant characters, including a specially drawn 'I' which appears slightly bolder than the other characters. More advanced readers and the 'Magic circle' and 'Little books' are set in Univers. In many cases the illustrations dominate the page, with type fitted in accordingly.

Helen Keenan-Church, **Reading 360: The Ginn reading programme, readers**, *I can hide*, (level 2, book 3), 1978
Illustrations: Rosie Evans
14 pp, 220 × 166 mm

Helen Keenan-Church, **Reading 360: The Ginn reading programme, readers**, *The park*, (level 3, book 1), 1978
Illustrations: Rosie Evans
14 pp, 220 × 166 mm

Priscilla M. Maynard, **Reading 360: The Ginn reading programme, magic circle books**, *Stop! Look!*, 1978
Illustrations: Joan Paley
16 pp, 195 × 195 mm

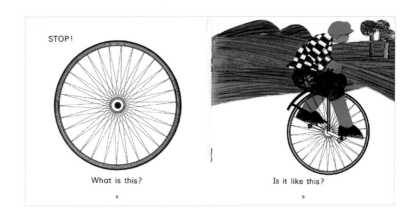

Barbara Mitchelhill, **Reading 360: The Ginn reading programme, little books**, *Come and play with me*, 1978
Illustrations: Sue Lisansky
12 pp, 157 × 164 mm

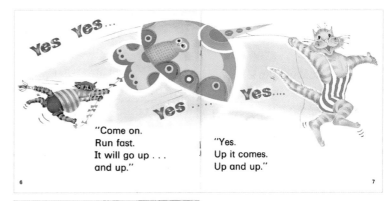

The 1960s and 1970s

The 1960s and 1970s

Sheila McCullagh, **One, two, three and away!**, St Albans: Hart-Davis Educational, 1979
[DTC]

'One, two, three and away!' is described as a 'context support' approach to teaching reading. It is based on two principles: that children 'should find all the books and materials interesting', and that the text, even in the earliest books, should be 'very easy and very carefully graded so that children gain confidence in their reading ability from the beginning'.

The early books in the series are set in various sizes of Gill Sans with infant characters, the more advanced ones in Baskerville.

Sheila McCullagh, **One, two, three and away!**
Pre-Reader 5: One, Two, Three,
Illustrations: Ferelith Eccles Williams
8 pp, 182 × 128 mm

Sheila McCullagh, **One, two, three and away!**
The cats' dance,
Illustrations: Ferelith Eccles Williams
32 pp, 215 × 152 mm

That night, when Jennifer went to bed,
she looked outside and saw the moon shining.
She looked at the garden wall,

Jim Rogerson and Ann Williams, **Crown reader,** *We live in the castle*, A. Wheaton & Co, 1980 [DTC]

Illustrations: Brian Heaton

8 pp, 210 × 148 mm

· A series of twelve 'mainline' readers and twelve 'supplementary' readers about the same group of characters.

· Typeset in 18-point Univers with infant characters.

· Unusually headings introduce the main text on each page.

· The text is consistently positioned below each illustration.

· The *Teacher's manual* notes that: 'Careful consideration has been given to the line breaks. Each unit of meaning has been presented on the same line, so that the child's eye movement from one line to the next does not destroy the meaning of the sentence.' (p. 1).

The King

I am the King.
I live in the castle.
The castle is big.
It is big and old.

2

The Queen

I am the Queen.
I live in the castle.
The castle is old.
It is old and big.

3

The baby

This is the baby.
The baby lives in the castle.
The castle is big.
It is big. It is old.

4

The big guard

I am a guard.
I am a big guard.
I live in the castle.
It is big. It is old.

5

I am the Queen.
I live in the castle.
The castle is old.
It is old and big.

On the sand

Book design for children's reading

Roderick Hunt, **Oxford reading tree**, Oxford University Press, 1986 [DTC]
Illustrations: Alex Brychta

The Oxford Reading Tree comprises a core of twenty-four story books in five stages. The books tell stories about a group of characters and their activities.

The early stages in the series use a handwritten font 'to simulate the handwriting done by the teacher'.

From Stage 4 the books are typeset in a specially designed version of Gill that includes educational characters. Many of the letters bear little resemblance to the original version of Gill Sans.

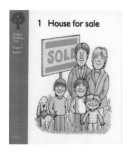

Roderick Hunt, **Oxford reading tree**, Stage 1. *What a bad dog!: a story about Floppy*, 1986
Illustrations: Alex Brychta
16 pp, 192 × 167 mm

Roderick Hunt, **Oxford reading tree**, Stage 4. *Book 1 House for sale*, 1986
Illustrations: Alex Brychta
16 pp, 192 × 167 mm

The 1980s onwards

Elizabeth Lawrence, **Open door**, *Robert has made a mess*, Hong Kong: Thomas Nelson & Sons, 1986 [DTC]

Illustrations: Malcolm Livingstone

16 pp, 210 × 144 mm

· A reading scheme in five stages with ten or twelve books in each stage. This one is from Stage 2.

· The typeface is highly customised, possibly achieved by combining typefaces rather than creating a new one. The text is set in Helvetica with single-bowl a's, but the normally square punctuation is replaced by round full stops and commas that resemble Times. The capital 'M' and small letter 'r' are replaced by characters more similar to Gill Sans. Because of careful judgement about the weight of characters, the overall appearance is quite harmonious.

· Note the speech bubble containing words relevant to the action in the picture.

· New words appear in very small type at the bottom of the pages where they occur.

Donna Bailey (ed.), Diana Perkins, Penny Hegarty, and Jean Chapman, **New way**, *Fat Pig's birthday and other stories*, Basingstoke: Macmillan Education, 1987 [DTC]

Illustrations: Elizabeth Haines, Nina O'Connell and Tony Kenyon

24 pp, 202 × 153 mm

- The 'New way' had its foundation in 'The gay way' series first published in the 1950s, and uses some of the same stories and characters.

- The teacher's books for the series contain a section on 'print, punctuation and illustrations' that draws on research, for example, by Bridie Raban on line endings.

- The series is typeset in a sanserif font with specially drawn characters, such as the 'i' and 't'.

- Different illustrators are used for each of the stories in the books.

The man sat down by a tree.
He was hot, so hot.
He went to sleep.
Zzzzzzz. Zzzzzzz. Zzzzzzz.

18

When he woke up
he had one cap on his head,
but that was all.
He looked and looked
for his caps.

19

Tom was in front.
He fell over.
Jenny went past.
Tom got up.
He went very fast.

8

Hello Tom, said his Dad.
You have jumped fast but
you have jumped back
to the start.

9

but that was all.
He looked and looked
for his caps.

Wendy Body (ed.), **Longman reading world**, Harlow: Longman Group, 1987 [DTC]

Longman reading world aims to make reading enjoyable through emphasis on stories and 'visual appeal'. It was organised in levels and at level 4 adopted an anthology approach to include poetry and non-fiction.

The teacher's book explained: 'Naturally, great care has been taken throughout the scheme regarding factors that affect readability. These include: syntax, vocabulary, layout, spacing, and size, density and clarity of type'.

Different typefaces were used in the book, along with handwritten letterforms.

Pat Edwards, **Longman reading world**, *Sadie spider strikes again*, 1987
Illustrations: Bucket
16 pp, 240 × 185 mm

Pat Edwards, **Longman reading world**, *Greedy pigs*, 1987
Illustrations: Maggie Ling
24 pp, 240 × 185 mm

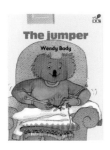

Wendy Body, **Longman reading world**, *The jumper*, 1987
Illustrations: Martina Selway
16 pp, 240 × 185 mm

Pat Edwards, **Longman reading world**, *The picnic*, 1987
Illustrations: Martina Selway
16 pp, 240 × 185 mm

Paul Groves, **Longman reading world**, *Garden rain*, 1987
Illustrations: Edward McLachlan
6 pp, 240 × 185 mm

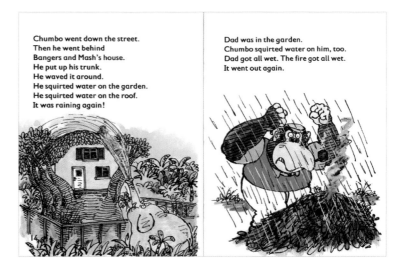

The 1980s onwards

The 1980s onwards

Pat Green (ed.), **Collins book bus**, *An oak tree*, London and Glasgow: Collins Educational, 1989 [DTC]

The 'book bus' comprises books in a wide variety of formats: paperback and hardback, in a range of sizes and extents from 8 to 48 pages.

The books were designed so that 'each stands alone' and a 'variety of typefaces and environmental print reflect the individual nature of each title'.

Serif and sanserif typefaces are used in many different configurations giving the books a 'trade' rather than a 'schoolbook ' feel.

Liz Byfield, **Collins book bus**, *An oak tree*, 1989
Illustrations: Jane Molineaux
16 pp, 160 × 135 mm

Some of the buried acorns are forgotten and lie in the ground through the winter.
10   11

The squirrels bury acorns in the wood, so they will have food for the winter.
8

The jays fly off to make their winter stores in the fields near the woods.
9

Tony Bradman, **Collins book bus**, *Peg-leg Pat the pirate*, 1992
Illustrations: Jacqueline East
8 pp, 136 × 160 mm

I'm Peg-Leg Pat the Pirate.
2

I sail the seven seas;
3

Mary Rayner, **Collins book bus**, *Rug*, 1990
Illustrations: Mary Rayner
32 pp, 230 × 180 mm

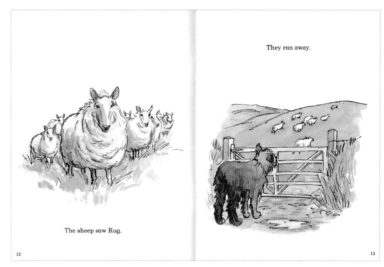

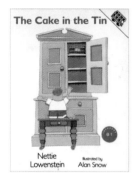

Nettie Lowenstein, **Collins book bus**, *The cake in the tin*, 1990
16 pp, 250 × 190 mm

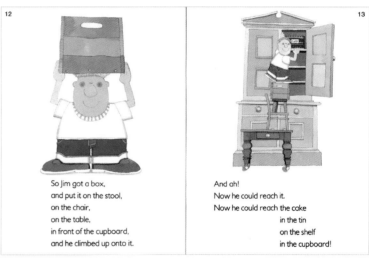

Sarah Garland, **Collins book bus**, *The seaside Christmas tree*, 1990
Illustrations: Sarah Garland
32 pp, 250 × 190 mm

The 1980s onwards

Richard Brown and Kate Ruttles (eds), **Cambridge reading**, Cambridge: Cambridge University Press, 1996 [DTC]

Cambridge reading comprises three levels: beginning to read, becoming a reader and towards independence, each with a balance of different text types and genres. The books were by new and established authors and illustrators and had little of the consistency and regularity of many earlier schemes.

One of the distinctive features was 'carefully controlled design features, including typeface, size and position of text.'

For their typeface Cambridge chose the rarely used Berthold Concorde, customising the 'd', 'f', 'g' and 'y'.

Richard Brown, **Cambridge reading**, *All by myself*, 1996
Illustrations: Gill Scriven
16 pp, 230 × 180 mm

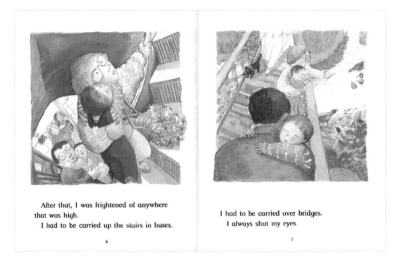

I had to be carried over bridges.
I always shut my eyes.

John Prater, **Cambridge reading**, *Nishal's box*, 1996
Illustrations: John Prater
24 pp, 230 × 180 mm

Book design for children's reading

Grace Hallworth, **Cambridge reading**, *Sleep tight*, 1996
Illustrations: Lisa Kopper
24 pp, 230 × 180 mm

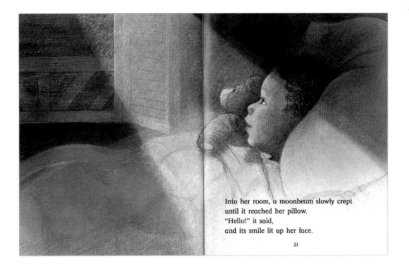

Into her room, a moonbeam slowly crept
until it reached her pillow.
"Hello!" it said,
and its smile lit up her face.

21

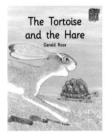

Gerald Rose, **Cambridge reading**, *The tortoise and the hare*, 1996
Illustrations: Gerald Rose
16 pp, 230 × 180 mm

The hare ran very fast.

6

The tortoise was very slow.

7

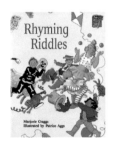

Marjorie Craggs, **Cambridge reading**, *Rhyming riddles*, 1996
Illustrations: Patrice Aggs
24 pp, 230 × 180 mm

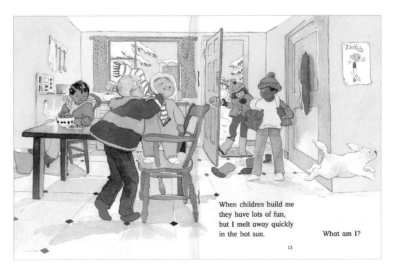

When children build me
they have lots of fun,
but I melt away quickly
in the hot sun.   What am I?

13

Conclusion

Since the end of the nineteenth century there have been many examples of exemplary typography and excellent illustration in books for teaching reading. These have anticipated and delivered the kind of reading experience that young children deserve and respond well to. There are also examples of ingenious though perhaps not very successful design solutions, or styles of illustration that are dull and not very engaging.

Some design features introduced at a particular time became accepted practice. The Ginn reading schemes in the 1920s, combined the use of a typeface believed to have characteristics helpful for children's reading with careful use of vertical and horizontal space, so that the pages appeared uncluttered and more welcoming than typical early twentieth-century readers that had pages full of type and illustrations. A second significant development was the alignment of content with a page or double page spread, typically in the form of an illustration and related text. Realisation that illustration was an important component of this kind of book led to the use of named illustrators for an entire series and as a result a significant element of a reading scheme brand. Some reading schemes stood out because they broke established conventions at a particular time; the Ginn series have already been mentioned but there were others, especially in the 1930s when some publishers used new sanserif typefaces for continuous text.

Alongside these developments there were a number of approaches, or experiments, that either failed to catch on or were one-off examples. The Initial Teaching Alphabet, and reading books that children could also write in are two examples, the first failing on pedagogic grounds and the second on practical and economic ones. Some trends, such as the use of a handwritten script for the text, were popular at particular periods of time, such as the concern by some teachers to replicate printscript in the 1920s and 1930s; and the use of handwriting to add informality and accessibility in the 'Ladybird key words reading scheme' in the 1960s and the early stages of the 'Oxford reading tree' in the 1980s.

Book design for teaching reading exemplifies well the relationship between context (the reader, the circumstances of use, the technological opportunities and constraints, historical precedent, pedagogy), and linguistic and graphic form. As has been shown, decisions about typography and layout were often made by compositors and printers who followed typesetting conventions for general book typography, and whose practice was sometimes influenced by the views of teachers. Robert Morss, writing in 1935, stressed the importance of the publisher 'who must design the bridge between the author and reader', synthesising the combined efforts of the typographer, printer, binder, papermaker, and artist-illustrator to produce a really good school-book.[83] The extent to which publishers did indeed assume this role is difficult to judge because of lack of evidence, specifically with regard to school-books, but it is certainly the case that major educational publishers in the latter decades of the twentieth century recognised the value of collaboration between author, illustrator, publisher and printer. In the 1980s, for example, 'Cambridge reading' involved a huge amount of preparatory work, including testing of the books in schools and obtaining feedback from children and teachers, as well as expert opinion and the usual concerns of the various departments within a large publishing house such as Cambridge University Press. Such attention to quality and making sure that the books were appropriate for use in schools is reminiscent of the aspirations of Hughes, McLean and Pinnock identified at the beginning of this account.

83. Morss, 'The neglected schoolbook', 1935, p. 11.

Select bibliography

Abercrombie, David, 'Augmenting the roman alphabet', *The Monotype Recorder*, vol. 42, no. 3, 1962–3, pp. 3–18.

Altick, Richard D., *The English common reader*. Chicago: University of Chicago Press, 1957.

Baines, Phil, *Puffin by design: 70 years of imagination 1940–2010*. London: Allen Lane, 2010.

Baldwin, Gertrude, *Patterns of sound: a book of alliterative verse. A method of learning to read successfully for beginners and reluctant readers*. London: The Chartwell Press, 1967.

Board of Education, *Report of the consultative committee on books in public elementary schools*. London: HMSO, 1928, pp. 1–27.

British Association for the Advancement of Science. *Report on the influence of school-books upon eyesight*. London: John Murray, 1913.

Buckingham, B. R., 'New data on the typography of textbooks', *Textbooks in American education. Thirtieth yearbook, Part II, of the National Society for the Study of Education*. Chicago: University of Chicago Press, 1931, pp. 93–125.

Bullock, Sir Alan, *A language for life, report of the Committee of Inquiry appointed by the Secretary of State for Education and Science under the chairmanship of Sir Alan Bullock*. London: HMSO, 1975.

Burroughs, George Edward Richard, *A study of the vocabulary of young children*. Edinburgh: Oliver & Boyd, 1957.

Burt, Cyril, 'The typography of children's books: a record of research in the UK', *Yearbook of Education*, 1960, pp. 242–56.

Coghill, Vera, 'Can children read familiar words set in unfamiliar type?', *Information Design Journal*, vol. 1, no. 4, 1980, pp. 254–60.

Dale, Nellie, *On the teaching of English reading with a running commentary on the Walter Crane Readers*. London: J. M. Dent & Co, 1898.

Daniels, J. C. and Hunter Diack. *The Royal Road Readers teachers' book*. London: Chatto and Windus, 1954.

Darton, F. J. Harvey, *Children's books in England: five centuries of social life,* 3rd edn revised by Brian Alderson. London and New Castle: British Library and Oak Knoll Press, 1982.

Dean, Joan, 'Words in Colour', in John Downing (ed.), *The first international reading symposium*. London: Cassell, 1966, pp. 74–91.

Dean, Joan, 'Second report on Words in Colour', in John Downing and A. Brown (eds), *The second international reading symposium*. London: Cassell, 1967, pp. 169–78.

Downing, John, *The i.t.a. reading experiment: three lectures on the research in infant schools with Sir James Pitman's Initial Teaching Alphabet*. London: Evans Brothers, 1964.

Downing, John, *The i.t.a. symposium: research report on the British experiment with i.t.a.* Slough: NFER, 1967.

Downing, John, 'Reform of the English writing-system', *The Penrose Annual*, vol. 61, 1968, pp. 102–6.

Edwards, Viv and Sue Walker, *Building bridges: multilingual resources for children*. Clevedon, Avon: Multilingual Matters, 1995.

Ellis, Alec, *A history of children's reading and literature*. Oxford: Pergamon Press, 1968.

Ellis, Alec, *Books in Victorian elementary schools*. London: The Library Association, 1971.

Goldsmith, Evelyn, *Research into illustration: an approach and a review*. Cambridge: Cambridge University Press, 1984.

Goldsmith, Evelyn, 'Learning from illustrations: factors in the design of illustrated educational books in general and for older infants', *Word and image*, vol. 2, no. 2, April–June, 1986, pp. 111–12.

Goldstrom, Joachim M., *Education: elementary education 1780–1900*. Newton Abbot: David & Charles, 1972.

Gunn, John, *The infant school: its principles and methods*. London: Thomas Nelson and Sons, 1906.

Hall, Jeremy, 'The initial teaching alphabet', *Eye*, 14, 2005, pp. 76–7.

Hedvall, A. and Bror Zachrisson, 'Children and their books', *The Penrose Annual*, vol. 56, 1962, pp. 59–66.

Heller, Steve, 'Typography for children' in S. Heller and K. Pomeroy (eds), *Design literacy: understanding graphic design*. New York: Allworth Press, 1997, pp. 108–11.

Hochuli, Jost and Robin Kinross, *Designing books: practice and theory*. London: Hyphen Press, 1996.

Holman, Valerie, *Print for victory: book publishing in England 1939–1945*. London: British Library, 2008.

Holmes, Heather and David Finkelstein (eds), *Thomas Nelson and Sons. Memories of an Edinburgh publishing house*. East Linton: Tuckwell Press, 2001.

Horner, P., 'The development of reading books in England from 1870', in G. Brooks and A. K. Pugh (eds), *Studies in the history of reading*. Reading: University of Reading and UKRA, 1984.

Huey, Edmund, *The psychology and pedagogy of reading with a review of the history of reading and writing and of methods, texts and hygiene in reading*. New York: Macmillan, 1908 [2nd edn 1968 MIT Press].

Hunt, Roderick, *Oxford reading tree. Teacher's guide 1*, London: Oxford University Press, 1986.

Jones, J. Kenneth, 'A research report on colour story reading', *The Journal of Typographic Research*, vol. 2, no. 1, 1968, pp. 53–8.

Jones, J. Kenneth, 'Phonetic colour reading', in J. Downing and A. Brown (eds), *Third international reading symposium*. London: Cassell, 1968, pp. 91–106.

Keir, Gertrude, 'The use of pictures as an aid to reading', *Reading*, 4, 1970, pp. 6–11.

Lawlor, Thomas, *Seventy years of textbook publishing: a history of Ginn and Company*. Boston: Ginn and Company, 1938.

Legros, Lucien A. and Grant, John C., *Typographical printing surfaces*. London: Longmans, Green & Co, 1916 (Section on 'Type, leading and length of line for school-books', pp. 157–60).

Lund, Ole, 'Knowledge construction in typography: the case of legibility research and the legibility of sans serif typefaces'. Unpublished PhD thesis, Department of Typography & Graphic Communication, University of Reading, 1999.

Mackay, D., B. Thompson and P. Schaub, *Breakthrough to literacy teacher's manual: the theory and practice of teaching initial reading and writing*. London: Schools Council Longman Group, 1970.

Mason, John H., 'The printing of children's books', *The Imprint*, vol. 2, no. 9, 1913, pp. 87–94.

McKee, Paul, M. Lucile Harrison, Annie McCowen and Elizabeth Lehr, *Teacher's manual for With Peter and Susan*, London: Thomas Nelson & Sons, [1955].

McKitterick, David, 'Changes in the look of the book' in *The Cambridge history of the book in Britain, vol. VI, 1830–1914*, Cambridge: Cambridge University Press, pp. 75–116.

McKitterick, David (ed.), *The Cambridge history of the book in Britain, volume VI, 1830–1914*, Cambridge: Cambridge University Press, 2009.

Meek, Margaret, *Learning to read*, London: Bodley Head, 1982.

Michael, Ian, *The teaching of English – from the sixteenth century to 1870*, Cambridge: Cambridge University Press, 1987.

Monotype, 'Annual or perennial? The problem of producing books for young readers', *Monotype Recorder*, vol. 43, no. 2, 1935, pp. 14–16.

Monotype, 'Learning to read', *Monotype Newsletter*, no. 64, 1961.

Monotype, *The Monotype Recorder*, vol. 42, no. 3, 1962–3 (devoted to the Pitman Augmented Alphabet).

Monotype, 'Amusing and instructive: old and new ways of learning to read', *Monotype Newsletter*, no. 88, 1971, pp. 2–5.

Moon, Cliff, *Individualised reading*. Reading: Reading and Language Information Centre, 1990s various editions.

Morss, Robert D., 'The neglected schoolbook', *Monotype Recorder*, vol. 34, no. 2, 1935, pp. 3–13.

Munro, Rona, *A teachers' manual for use with the Janet and John reading course*. Welwyn: James Nisbet & Co, 1954.

Musgrave, Peter, 'Readers in Victoria, 1896–1968: the Victorian readers', *Paradigm*, 16, May 1955, pp. 1–12.

National Book League, *Textbook design exhibition 1966: catalogue of an exhibition of books published between May 1962 and May 1965*. London: National Book League, 1966.

Newsholme, Arthur and Walter C. Pakes, *School hygiene: the laws of health in relation to school life*. London: Swan Sonnenscheim & Co, 1904.

Obrist, Cecilia and P. M. Pickard, 'Time of reading', *Teachers' manual*, London: Ginn, 1967.

Philip, Hugh and Judith Guyen, 'Innovation in reading', *Experiments and innovations in education*, 3, Paris: UNESCO, 1973.

Pitman, Sir James, 'Learning to read with the augmented roman alphabet, *The Penrose Annual*, vol. 56, 1962, pp. 54–8.

Price, Hugh, 'Lo, it is my ox!: reading books and reading in New Zealand schools 1877–1900, *Paradigm*, 12 December 1993, pp. 1–14.

Raban, Bridie, 'Text display effects on the fluency of young readers', *Journal of Reading Research*, vol. 5, no. 1, 1982, pp. 7–28.

Raban, Bridie, 'Survey of teachers' opinions: children's books and handwriting styles', in D. Dennis (ed.), *Reading: meeting children's special needs*, London: Heinemann, 1984, pp. 123–9.

Reynolds, Linda and Sue Walker, '"You can't see what the words say": word spacing and letter spacing in children's reading books', *Journal of Research in Reading*, vol. 27, no. 1, 2004, pp. 87–98.

Reynolds, Linda, Sue Walker and Alison Duncan, 'Children's responses to line spacing in early reading books or 'Holes to tell you which line you're on', *Visible Language*, vol. 40, no. 3, 2006, pp. 246–67.

Salisbury, Martin and Morag Styles, *Children's picture books: the art of visual storytelling*. London: Laurence King, 2012.

Sassoon, Rosemary, 'A typeface with a special purpose', *Linotype Letterbox*, no. 6, 1991, pp. 10–11.

Sassoon, Rosemary, 'Through the eyes of a child: perception and type design' in Rosemary Sassoon (ed.), *Computers and typography*, Oxford: Intellect Books, 1993, pp. 150–77.

Schonell, Fred, *The Happy Venture teacher's manual*, London: Oliver & Boyd, 1945.

Schonell, Fred, *The psychology and teaching of reading*, London: Oliver & Boyd, 1945.

Shaw, Edward Richard, *School hygiene*. London: Macmillan & Co, 1902.

Shaw, Paul, 'The Century family' in Charles Bigelow, Paul Hayden Duensing and Linnea Gentry (eds), *Fine print on type*. San Francisco: Bedford Arts, 1989.

Smith, Jessica and Helen Watkins, 'An investigation into some aspects of the illustration of primary school books', unpublished report, Department of Typography & Graphic Communication, University of Reading, 1972.

Southward, John, *Modern printing: a handbook*. London: Raithby, Lawrence & Company, 1898.

Stiff, Paul, 'Showing a new world in 1942: the gentle modernity of Puffin Picture Books, *Design Issues*, Autumn 2007, vol. 23, no. 4, pp. 22–38.

Stray, Christopher and Gillian Sutherland, 'Mass markets: education' in David McKitterick (ed.), *The Cambridge history of the book in Britain, vol. VI 1830–1914*, Cambridge: Cambridge University Press, 2009.

Thomas, David, 'School books and their typography', *Printing Review*, vol. 13, 1934, pp. 5–8.

Tinker, Miles A., 'Print for children's text books', *Education*, 80, 1, 1959, pp. 37–40.

Tinker, Miles A., *Bases for effective reading*. Ames: Iowa State University Press, 1965.

Tinker, Miles A., 'Suitable typography for beginners in reading', *Education*, 88, 4, 1968, pp. 317–20.

Twyman, Michael, 'The bold idea: the use of bold-looking types in the nineteenth century', *Journal of the Printing Historical Society*, 1993, 22, pp. 107–14 3.

Twyman, Michael, 'The emergence of the graphic book in the nineteenth century' in R. Myers and M. Harris (eds), *A millennium of the book*. Winchester: St Paul's Bibliographies, 1994, pp. 135–80.

Twyman, Michael, *Printing 1770–1970 an illustrated history of its development and uses in England*, London: The British Library, 1998 (2nd edn).

Twyman, Michael, 'The illustration revolution' in David McKitterick (ed.), *The Cambridge history of the book in Britain, vol. VI 1830–1914*. Cambridge: Cambridge University Press, 2009, pp. 117–43.

Venezky, Richard L., 'A history of the American reading textbook', *Elementary School Journal*, vol. 87, no. 3, 1987, pp. 246–65.

Venezky, Richard L., 'From the Indian primer to Dick and Jane: an introduction to the UPA American primers collection' in *American primers: guide to the microfiche collection*. Bethesda, MD: University Publications of America, 1990.

Venezky, Richard L., 'The history of reading research', in D. P. Pearson, R. Barr, M. L. Kamil and P. Mosenthal, *Handbook of reading research*, vol. 1, London: Longman, 1984, pp. 3–38.

Walker, Sue, Viv Edwards and Ruth Blacksell, 'Designing bilingual books for children', *Visible Language*, vol. 30, no. 3, 1996, pp. 368–83.

Walker, Sue and Linda Reynolds, 'Serifs, sans serifs and infant characters in children's reading books', *Information Design Journal + Document Design*, vol. 11, no. 2/3, 2002/3, pp. 106–2.

Walker, Sue, 'The books that nobody sees: typography in children's reading books', *Baseline*, no. 48, 2005, pp. 25–32.

Walker, Sue, *The songs letters sing: typography and children's reading*. Reading: National Centre for Language and Literacy, 2005.

Walker, Sue, 'Letterforms for handwriting and reading: print script and sanserifs in early twentieth-century England', *Typography Papers* 7, London: Hyphen Press, 2007, pp. 81–114.

Walker, Sue, 'Describing the design of children's books: an analytical approach', *Visible Language*, vol. 46, no. 3, 2012, pp. 182–201.

Warde, Beatrice, 'Improving the compulsory book', *The Penrose Annual*, vol. 44, 1950, pp. 37–40.

Warde, Beatrice, 'The making of children's books', *The Times Literary Supplement*, 24 November, 1927. Reprinted in part in *The Monotype Recorder*, vol. 44, no. 1, 1970, p. 39.

Watts, Lynne and John Nisbet, *Legibility in children's books: a review of research*. Slough: NFER Publishing Company, 1974.

Williamson, Hugh, *Methods of book design: the practice of an industrial craft*. London: Oxford University Press, 1966 (2nd edn) and 3rd edn published by Yale University Press, 1983.

Willows, Dale M., Diane Borwick, and Maureen Hayvren, 'The content of school readers' in G. E. MacKinnon and T. G. Waller (eds), *Reading research: advances in theory and practice*, vol. 2, New York: Academic Press, 1981, pp. 97–175.

Yule, Valerie, 'The design of print for children: sales-appeal and user-appeal', *Reading*, vol. 22, no. 2, 1988, pp. 96–105.

Zachrisson, Bror, 'Some experiments with children regarding the readability of printed text', *Research Bulletin*, 9, Stockholm: University of Stockholm, Institute of Education, 1956.

Zachrisson, Bror, *Studies in the legibility of printed text*. Stockholm: Almqvist and Wiksell, 1965.

Appendix

Extracts from the British Association for the Advancement of Science, *Report on the influence of school-books upon eyesight*, London: John Murray, 1913.

The headings in the left-hand column are the sub-headings used in a section of the report entitled 'Hygienic requirements with which school-books should conform'.

The psychology of the reading process	'The trained reader generally recognises whole words and phrases at a glance. It is therefore important that the process of beginners should be made as easy as possible towards the recognition of word-wholes and phrase-wholes by the use of type suitable in character and judiciously spaced. The best type for isolated letters is not necessarily the best for word-wholes, and attention must be given to the comparative legibility of letters as seen in context.' p. 9
Workmanship	'It frequently happens that much of the good effect of well-selected type, paper, &c., is neutralised by inefficient workmanship.' p. 9
Paper	'The paper should be without gloss. Glazed paper is trying to the eyes by reasons of reflections which are apt to interfere with binocular vision. Pure white paper gives the greatest contrast with the ink, and therefore a paper which is white or slightly toned towards cream-colour is to be preferred under average conditions of class-room illumination. A hard-wearing paper of suitable quality should be used, as a soft paper has two defects —(1) it is readily soiled, (2) the surface is easily rubbed off and the detritus is injurious. The surface should be fairly smooth, because a rough-surfaced paper necessitates a heavy impression in order that the unbroken surface of each letter may appear, which impression is liable to cause a still rougher surface on the other side of the sheet.' pp. 9–10
	'The print of one side must not show through from the other, and the printing must not affect the evenness of the surface of the other side.' p. 10
	This extract about paper is a good example of the collation of the views of psychologists, printers and teachers.
Binding	'Books should be stitched with thread. Books should open flat and should not require the restraint of the hand to keep them so; stabbing or clipping should therefore be avoided. If not flat, the convex surface of the page gives rise to eye strain.' p. 10

Illustrations	'it is important to recollect that children are only confused by elaborate or complex pictures. Bold, firm treatment of a few objects is appropriate alike to their visual powers and to their understanding. From this point of view line blocks from pen-and-ink drawings are preferable to half-tone blocks from photographs or from wash-drawings. The pictures should be of a good size, and the printed text should not extend in narrow lines at the side.' p. 11
Ink	'The ink should be a good black, and it is important to secure a proper, sufficient, and even distribution of it over the whole page. The use of coloured inks for reading matter is strongly to be deprecated, especially the use of more than one colour on a page.' p. 11
	Was this a direct reference to the use of colour in 'The Dale readers', which were widely used in schools at the time?
Mode of printing	'The ordinary text of school-books which are intended for continuous reading should not be printed in double columns.' p. 12
Character of type	'The type should be clean-cut and well-defined. Condensed or compressed type should not be used, as breadth is even more important than height. The contrast between the finer and heavier strokes should not be great, for hair strokes are difficult to see. On the other hand, a very heavy-faced type suffers in legibility through diminution of the white inter-spaces, as, for example, when the space in the upper half of the **e** is reduced to a white dot. In an ideal type ... it is easy to discriminate between **e, c** and **o**, between **i** and **l**, and between **h** and **k**; and to recognise **m, nn, nu, nv, w, in**. The general form of the letter should be broad and square rather than elongated vertically; thus the letter **o** should approach the circular shape.' p. 12
	'The upper half of the word or letter is usually more important for perception than is the lower half, because the upper half of most letters has a more distinctive shape than the lower.' p. 13
	'With reference to the question of 'modern-face' versus 'old-face' design for type, the Committee is not prepared to advise the use of either to the exclusion of the other, good and bad varieties of both styles being present in use. Great contrast between the thick and thin strokes is a serious defect which often appears in 'modern face'. It is claimed for the 'modern face' that the letters are more legible, and it may be conceded that failure to provide the minimum height of the short letters is more frequent in the 'old face'. p. 13
	'The advocates of the 'old face' contend that the 'modern face' letters remain isolated, whereas the letters of the 'old face' flow more naturally into words; thus the form of the word and its meaning are apprehended smoothly. It is also claimed that the basic design for the 'old face' is of higher aesthetic merit.' p. 13
	The typefaces used in the examples in the report (see an example on p. 24) were named as Old Style Antique, Old Style, Old Face and Modern.

Character of type [continued]	'Italic, being less easy to read than ordinary type of the same size, should be used sparingly.' p. 13
Size of type-faces and their vertical and horizontal separation	The size of type-face is the most important factor in the influence of books upon vision. Legibility depends mainly on the height and breadth of the short letters, for the larger the type and the further from the eyes can it be read with ease, and it is of the first importance to induce the young reader to keep a sufficient distance between eyes and book. Children under seven years old should be able to lean back in their seats and read from the book propped up on the far side of the desk.' pp. 13–14
	'space between the lines should vary in proportion to the size of type. Too little space is a source of fatigue in reading, for it involves difficulty in passing from the end of a line to the beginning of the line below. Very wide space, on the other hand, has no advantage as regards legibility, and involves waste of paper and undesirable increase in the size of the book.' p. 15
Length of the line	'The length of the line is important in a school book intended for continuous reading. Other things being equal, the longer the line the greater the excursions of the eyes and the greater the difficulty in passing from one line to the next. Very short lines, on the other hand, demand too frequent a change of direction in the movement of the eyes.' p. 15
	'Unusual separation [letter spaced in the original] of letters should be avoided. For beginners lines should not end in the middle of a word; the whole word should be carried to the next line and not be hyphened.' p. 16
	'Good margins are restful to the eye, and are well worth their slight cost … It should be considered a defect in a school-book if the width of fore-edge is less than half an inch, or of back-edge less than three-eights of an inch, at any page of the book.' p. 16

Index

Page numbers in *italics* refer to illustrations.

Series' titles are in single quotes and followed by the publisher's name in parentheses.